"Over my 50-year career as a transformational change facilitator, I've witnessed the acceleration of the speed and complexity of organizational adaptation. This book is the best consolidation and codification of best practices for [a different approach to strategic planning and implementation] that I've seen. [The authors] make the Strategic Doing methodology clear and provide a manageable roadmap that makes the methodology easy to apply ... just in time to address the largest speed and complexity challenges mankind has known."

Bob Sadler, CEO of Sadler Consulting, executive coach and authority on change leadership and executive presence

"Don't even bother reading all those other books on leadership and strategy. I know because I've written a number of them. *Strategic Doing* is THE source to understand how leadership and strategy are changing in this age of speed and complexity. What makes this book more important are the ten practical skills that you and your colleagues can learn to become masterful at leading in a disruptive age."

Jay Conger, chaired professor of Leadership Studies at Claremont McKenna College and author of The High Potentials Advantage

"Over the past 30 years, I have been traveling the world for *60 Minutes*. One trend is clear. The challenges we face are growing in complexity. The best way to address these challenges is through human ingenuity unleashed through collaboration. This book illuminates that path. Recommended."

Bob Anderson, producer, 60 Minutes (CBS)

"After 12 years in public office, working on the complex, systemic, and interwoven challenges of poverty, crime, health disparity, and economic development, I can say that our nation desperately needs the guidance provided by *Strategic Doing*. At a time of global change and national strife, the lessons in this book not only provide a path for multiorganizational success, they represent a practical, nonpartisan formula to preserve our American democracy."

Lawrence Morrissey, mayor, Rockford, Illinois 2005–2017

"Ed Morrison has mastered the art of making progress happen in a complex, change-resistant world. Now he and his colleagues have assembled decades of hard-won lessons into an easy-to-assimilate book – which is great news for every enemy of chaos, confusion, and inertia."

John D. Donahue, faculty chair of Harvard's Masters in Public Policy program and author of Collaborative Governance

"If you want to *do something* to make your community better but worry, 'I'll need a grant' or 'I'll need a powerful board of advisors,' stop worrying and start doing! Strategic Doing requires *no money, no powerful CEOs*, and *no one's permission*. It's a simple-to-understand process that any group can use to take the resources they have and launch innovative and impactful projects. I use it with my clients and am consistently blown away by what people like you and me can do with Strategic Doing."

Rebecca Ryan, futurist, economist, and author of Regeneration: A Manifesto for America's Next Leaders

"When our foundation was looking for a tool to offer to the rural communities we serve, Strategic Doing emerged as the right vehicle. The agility of the process enables a group of 5 or a group of 50 to bring forth an idea, divide the workload, determine the feasibility, and when appropriate, foster the implementation. Our communities have been encouraged by increased participation in civic activity from a broad spectrum of ages."

Betsy Wearing, coordinator of Communications, Programs, and New Initiatives, Dane G. Hansen Foundation

"An important evolution is taking place among US land-grant universities. ... The learning, discovery, and engagement taking place on our campuses today is now pointing us to new approaches to the economic challenges facing society. This valuable book builds on that tradition through the new discipline of Strategic Doing to achieve higher and more productive levels of collaboration. ... Anyone interested in solving such problems more effectively, faster, and more collaboratively will find this book a welcome treasure."

Martin Jischke, former president, Purdue University

"This is a book about Strategic **Doing**. It not only consolidates years of real experience but is also written in a style that is fully consistent with the title: action focused. ... Because of the integration of the broad base of experience with the science of ecology, cybernetics, and complexity, this book shows a depth beyond expectation, considering how hands-on and practical this proven approach is."

Peter Robertson, executive lecturer and research fellow, Nyenrode Business University (The Netherlands)

"Applying deep underpinnings in social science research, Lean/Agile experimentation, and refinement through rigorous practice, the Strategic Doing founders have created a framework to define and execute strategy for our time. ... This book is for anyone or any organization that wants to tackle a 'big hairy audacious problem' with effective, complex collaboration. "

Patricia Sheehan, Agile Transformation lead and coach, AstraZeneca Agile Centre of Excellence

"Strategic Doing is the most impressive and effective way to get things done in our community. It allows everyone an opportunity for input and provides clarity of vision, mission, purpose, and tasks upon which we have all agreed. If we continue to work together, there is no limit to our achievements."

Macke Mauldin, president, Bank Independent

"As someone who leads a complex organization, I am always looking for new approaches to how I work. Learning to be proactive and truly collaborative is what the Strategic Doing method has taught me. Strategic Doing is not just for the workplace but can easily be applied to all areas of life that involve people coming together for a common goal. These are simple and well-supported skills that anyone can employ in their work and life to make a tangible difference."

Stephen Jennings, senior vice president, Rady Children's Hospital; executive director, Rady Children's Hospital Foundation

"The challenges we face today – in our communities, in the economy, and in society as a whole – are far too complex to be ameliorated by the same simple approaches to planning and implementation that we've used in the past. This book provides a road map to the future of strategy, and to a better world."

Jim Woodell, former vice president for Economic Development and Community Engagement, Association of Public and Land-Grant Universities; convener, Collaborative for Insight and Impact

The convergence of the physical and digital worlds, especially in manufacturing, presents unprecedented opportunity for the creation of transformational value. With all the chess pieces on the table, there are a seemingly unlimited number of opportunities. ... [L]eaders need the skills and insights presented in this book. *Strategic Doing* should be required reading for every leader charting a pathway forward.

Don Cooper, vice president, PTC/Global Rockwell Alliance

"Strategic Doing is a straightforward vehicle to get to a decision and action, very quickly, with busy people. In an era where diversity and collaboration are critical to success, it can be done quickly and efficiently. ... It is time tested, and I recommend this book with enthusiasm!"

Charles Van Rysselberge, president (retired), Oklahoma City Chamber of Commerce, Charleston (South Carolina) Chamber of Commerce

"Speed and agility are hallmarks of successful companies. In the world of software engineering, agile methodology and design thinking have become ubiquitous tactical systems for getting to better results in less time when faced with complex challenges. Yet, a gap remains between this agile methodology at the tactical level and the way leaders often think in setting direction for their organizations. This book addresses that gap and should be required reading for every organizational leader."

Kenneth Johnson, CEO, Blue Sentry Group

"For those involved in strategic planning and management across corporate, government, universities, and community organizations, Strategic Doing provides three key advantages. It addresses the fundamental flaws that have emerged in the application of traditional strategy and planning within a whole new environment. Secondly, it provides a simple, logical, low cost, and low risk way of getting the right things to happen quickly and – thirdly – it works!"

Emeritus Professor Michael Hefferan, University of the Sunshine Coast
(Queensland, Australia)

"After 30-plus years as a leader in the hospitality industry, I've realized collaboration is a much-needed skill that is often challenging to implement in a fast-paced service environment. As the founder of a company with completely remote-based employees, clients all over the world, and multiple projects happening on a daily basis, learning the art of collaboration is something that is crucial to our success – yet something not taught in most workplaces or universities. [T]his book is a must read for anyone who wants to succeed in business, or, for that matter, in life today!"

Caryl Helsel, founder and CEO, Dragonfly Strategists

"Today's communities, geopolitical regions, economies, and societies face many highly complex challenges. Effective solutions to these challenges require that the leaders of organizations charged with addressing them – be they educational, governmental, nongovernmental, or private – must work across traditional organizational, cultural, and geopolitical boundaries. Strategic Doing, with its ten skills to developing effective networks, is a much-needed 'perspective changer' on strategy and leadership."

Vic Lechtenberg, former provost, Purdue University

It doesn't matter the context in which you are operating, whether you find yourself in a corporate, government, or nonprofit space – if you're bringing twentieth century solutions to twenty-first century problems, you will not have the agility to effect meaningful change. Strategic Doing is a twenty-first century solution. This book provides the reader with a set of practices for tapping into the resources of loosely connected networks and helping your organization move forward quickly. … Change is the new constant. This book will help you successfully embrace that change.

Will Samson, Organizational Change Management, General Dynamics
Information Technology

"Everyone agrees that complex problems require complex solutions. ... How ironic is it that the answer to this collaboration-complexity nexus is something very *simple*: the ten skills of Strategic Doing. Strategic Doing takes an asset-based approach. However, the identification of assets is a hollow victory if those assets are not mobilized. It provides the skills to catalyze this mobilization, leading to two important outcomes: problems are solved and the human capital of the participants is simultaneously enhanced. Can there be a better win-win scenario?"

Sam Cordes, professor emeritus and cofounder, Purdue Center for
Regional Development

"As many warn that our technology might serve to isolate us, the authors offer real, all-hands-on-deck hope: a daring and wonderful proposition for us to work and think *together* – and accomplish things others might once have deemed formidable in the extreme. ... I like to tell kids they can build a better future, and paint a portrait of what that could look like, but they are actually charting the course, a way to get there. For all of us, I hope the world listens and *does* likewise."

Noah Knox Marshall, author, Dax Zander: Sea Patrol

"Dealing with intractable challenges in your family, organization, or community? Look no further. This book, replete with clear guidance and real-life examples, shows you how to work with others to implement practical solutions that transform big wishes into reality."

Eleanor Bloxham, founder and CEO, The Value Alliance and
Corporate Governance Alliance

"[Our] manufacturing ecosystem is much stronger and much more collaborative as a result of the skills taught in Strategic Doing. Montana's successful entrepreneurs depend on agile strategies where all manufacturers collaborate for mutual benefit. It is great that these skills are being brought together in this important book."

Paddy Fleming, director, Montana Manufacturing Extension Center, part
of the National Institute of Standards and Technology's Manufacturing
Extension Partnership (NIST MEP)

strategic **doing**

TEN SKILLS FOR **AGILE LEADERSHIP**

EDWARD MORRISON, SCOTT HUTCHESON, ELIZABETH NILSEN,

JANYCE FADDEN, AND NANCY FRANKLIN

Published by John Wiley & Sons, Inc., Hoboken, New Jersey.

Published simultaneously in Canada.

For general information on our other products and services or for technical support, please contact our Customer Care Department within the United States at (800) 762-2974, outside the United States at (317) 572-3993 or fax (317) 572-4002.

Wiley publishes in a variety of print and electronic formats and by print-on-demand. Some material included with standard print versions of this book may not be included in e-books or in print-on-demand. If this book refers to media such as a CD or DVD that is not included in the version you purchased, you may download this material at http://booksupport.wiley.com. For more information about Wiley products, visit www.wiley.com.

Library of Congress Cataloging-in-Publication Data

Names: Morrison, Edward, author.
Title: Strategic doing : ten skills for agile leadership / Edward Morrison
  [and four others].
Description: Hoboken, New Jersey : John Wiley & Sons, Inc., [2019] | Includes
  bibliographical references and index. |
Identifiers: LCCN 2018060350 (print) | LCCN 2019001681 (ebook) | ISBN
  9781119578406 (ePub) | ISBN 9781119578611 (ePDF) | ISBN 9781119578666
  (hardcover)
Subjects: LCSH: Strategic alliances (Business) | Business networks. |
  Public-private sector cooperation. | Leadership.
Classification: LCC HD69.S8 (ebook) | LCC HD69.S8 M673 2019 (print) | DDC
  658.4/012—dc23
LC record available at https://lccn.loc.gov/2018060350

Cover Design: Wiley
Cover Image: © David Allen Moss

Printed in the United States of America

V10009037_032819

This book is dedicated to the remarkable Strategic Doing community that now stretches across the globe. You inspire us.

CONTENTS

FOREWORD

I've been waiting for this book all my life. Strategic Doing answers so many questions I have on how cultural organizations can band together to be part of the solution in addressing society's most complex issues.

I was a witness to and participant in this approach when I met Ed Morrison in Youngstown, Ohio, working with a group of socially committed citizens, each determined to work to reinvigorate a once-thriving community. In one short hour he had each of us identify and unlock our assets, come up with a plausible group plan, and determine a course of action moving forward, agreeing to meet again 30 days from that moment.

Now we have the book that details 50 years (between its five coauthors) of work, showing how Strategic Doing has been catalytic in revitalizing communities, cities, industries, and sectors all across the country.

Strategic Doing is precisely what we need at this moment. In a fast-changing world, filled with disruption, with institutions not equipped to absorb or deal with the pace of change, here is a way of thinking and acting – an agile strategy that makes collaboration take place at the necessary speed for social good.

Yo-Yo Ma
December 31, 2018
Arlington, Massachusetts

INTRODUCTION

Long before Flint, Michigan faced a water crisis, residents in the most distressed neighborhoods of that city confronted another challenge: teenage homicides. In 2010, a record 66 people were killed in Flint, a city of just more than 100,000 – mostly young African American men (for comparison, the national homicide rate is 4.9 per 100,000). Tendaji Ganges, Bob Brown, and Kenyetta Dotson came together with their Flint neighbors to pursue a traditional approach to addressing the problem: they applied for a federal grant. When their grant proposal was turned down, they decided to explore other options. Using the skills outlined in this book, they began building new networks to reclaim their neighborhoods. These leaders, joined by a handful of others, began focusing on the assets they had within their own networks to come up with new solutions to the challenges of youth violence. When the water crisis hit Flint a few years later, this new network of civic leaders committed to Strategic Doing[1] did not focus on protests (although as individuals, each of them participated in events and made their voices heard). Instead, they organized food trucks to bring fresh fruits and vegetables into their neighborhoods. Why? Because fresh fruits and vegetables mitigate the impact of lead poisoning. They did not wait around for others, and, most importantly, they were not paralyzed by a lack of funding. As one of the leaders later put it, "Strategic Doing broke our grant addiction. We thought we couldn't do anything without a grant." Bob Brown, a member of this Flint core team, explained it this way: "Strategic Doing gives us the power to change our lives, our neighborhoods, and our communities."

We will explore the remarkable story of these leaders in Flint later. Let's now turn our attention to Elizabeth Taylor, who manages the Space Biology program in NASA's Division of Space Biosciences. She focuses on guiding NASA's research investments to explore the impact of microgravity on fundamental biological processes. She is part of a team faced with the challenge of developing scientific and technology foundations needed to support safe and productive human exploration of space. The team's work focuses on cell biology and animal research. In addition to managing these programs, Elizabeth and her colleagues face challenges in building collaborations with the Human Research Program in NASA, which focuses on managing human space travel. Both the Space Biology Program and the Human Research Program are part of NASA's Division of Space Life and Physical Sciences. Like most government bureaucracies, the scientists and engineers within these two programs know each other, but collaborating is difficult: everyone is busy, and the pressures to perform are relentless. No one has enough time. So, when Elizabeth was given the responsibility of convening both the Space Biology Program and the Human Research Program to look for points of intersection and collaboration, she turned to Strategic Doing. Over a couple of days in Northern California, using the skills outlined in this book, she and her team guided conversations that led to the identification of a number of opportunities for complex collaborations, as well as taking the first steps in those collaborations, all in the matter of a few hours.

Now let's turn to the challenges faced by one of the nation's premiere aerospace and defense companies interested in securing new contracts with the US Navy. The Department of Defense recently introduced a requirement for its program managers to embed predictive maintenance in critical equipment systems, to increase operational readiness and reliability while reducing ownership cost and equipment downtime. At its simplest, predictive maintenance (also called condition-based maintenance, or CBM) means that there is a system in place that predicts machine failures before they happen.

Like all companies that compete on innovation, this firm is often faced with the "buy, build, or partner" choice when making strategic decisions about technology development. "Buy" was not an option, as a CBM solution was not available "off the shelf." "Build" is becoming harder for American defense contractors; recent changes to defense acquisition rules are squeezing out resources available for research and development, making that alternative impractical. Partnering was the best option. The company needed to identify technology companies capable of providing this expertise, rapidly perform a due-diligence assessment, and engineer a complex collaboration with these companies to generate a proof of concept. Using the skills outlined in this book, the company convened a series of four workshops engaging 90 companies, forming a collaboration to begin building a CBM solution. The CEO of one of the small technology companies involved in the process declared in the wrap-up meeting, "I've worked with large companies trying to do open innovation, but the Strategic Doing process is unique. This is the most clear and concise open innovation process I've seen."

Compare these examples to the meetings, planning processes, and committees you've found yourself on lately. Are you satisfied with the effectiveness of those gatherings, or do you feel like your time is too often wasted, important issues go unaddressed, and there's little follow-up? You may even be in charge of the discussions, and you too are frustrated.

OUR PROMISE

The issues faced by these teams are, on the face of it, quite different. Your own organization's concerns are probably different still. And yet, a common thread runs through them the need to find new ways to work together to tackle big challenges. This book will explain how we can navigate the world of complex challenges by strengthening our shared skills of collaboration. To most people, collaboration is just a word tossed around all too quickly. After reading this book, you will see that true collaboration runs much deeper than that. It is a set of ten shared skills that we call *Strategic Doing*. Anyone can learn these skills. We've taught them to (among others) scientists, engineers, business executives, high school students, healthcare practitioners, community activists, university administrators, local government officials, start-up entrepreneurs, and workforce and economic development professionals. We will explain these skills and illustrate how each of them is used as part of effective collaboration. We will also provide you with some background on the research that supports each of these skills.

Each of the skills on its own can make a tremendous impact on the effectiveness of the groups you're already involved with. Beyond that, they can be assembled into a process for building a complex collaboration from the ground up. You will see that although the skills may sound simple, they are not easy. Mastering the skills takes practice.

There is one more catch: in our experience, we've found that no one is really good at all ten skills. That is one reason, among others, that you need a diverse team to tackle a complex challenge. We'll have more to say about this in the closing chapter.

WHY ARE WE CONFIDENT? THE BACKSTORY OF OUR WORK

What makes us so confident that we can deliver on the promise we are making to you? To answer that question, we need to tell you more about how Strategic Doing came to be. Strategic Doing began in a parking garage in Oklahoma City in 1993. Back then, before the bombing that made the city famous around the globe, Oklahoma City was facing down a decade of stagnation. Oil prices had collapsed, and the city had yet to recover from a serious banking collapse a decade before. The Oklahoma City mayor, Ron Norick, and the Oklahoma City Chamber were busy planning a major renaissance through a multimillion-dollar infrastructure investment, called MAPS (Metropolitan Area Projects). Funded by a sales tax increase, MAPS generated over $400 million to build nine projects, including an arena, a renovated convention center, and a baseball stadium.

Investments in infrastructure, although needed, are not enough to turn around an economy. Only when the private sector has enough confidence to invest can a city's economy prosper. But how does a city trigger private investment? At the invitation of Charles Van Rysselberge, then-president of the Chamber of Commerce, Ed Morrison went to Oklahoma City to answer that question. He began work on a strategy for the Chamber (which at the time was located within a concrete bunker of a parking garage). Charles and Ed assembled a small core team of entrepreneurial civic leaders. The team included Clay Bennett, who later became a major force in moving an NBA basketball team from Seattle to Oklahoma City, and Burns Hargis, who later became president of Oklahoma State University.

A seasoned economic development consultant, Ed was arriving fresh on the heels of a number of engagements using traditional strategic planning models. He was increasingly convinced that these approaches, which relied on a costly linear process of analysis and execution of plans laid out many years into the future, simply did not work (for reasons we explain in Chapter 1). To complement MAPS, Ed proposed a new and (until then) untested approach. He suggested that the Chamber think of their strategy more like open source software development (a discipline that was then just emerging): a continuous iteration of experiments to figure out "what works" – what is now called an *agile* process. Ed's core team came up with seven strategic initiatives, all designed to leverage additional private sector investment in the city. They called this portfolio *Forward Oklahoma City: A New Agenda*.

In trying to adopt this new approach, the central problem faced by the team turned out to be this: How do you design and guide complex collaborations in open, loosely connected networks when no one can tell anyone else what to do? Developing a new way of working together as they went, the first sprouts of success in Oklahoma City began to appear in about three or four years – including a hiatus of a year or so in the immediate aftermath of the 1995 bombing. By 2000, the combination of MAPS and Forward Oklahoma City had triggered an additional $403 million in private investment, including $27 million in technology-based companies. Today, Oklahoma City has a dynamic economy, and the Chamber is continuing to build out new initiatives based on these original principles.

Here's one other metric of their success. In 1993, the only hotel downtown, the Medallion, rarely had more than a handful of guests (indeed, on some days Ed was convinced that he was the only guest in the only downtown hotel in the capital of Oklahoma). At night, downtown streets were too deserted and dangerous for a guest to venture out to find the one or two restaurants that might be open. The historic Skirvin Hotel, boarded up, served as a reminder of economic collapse. If you had asked civic leaders back then what should be done with the Skirvin, the dominant opinion would have been, "Tear it down." Now, fast forward to today. Oklahoma City has 18 downtown hotels, and the Skirvin has become a crown jewel.

In 2010, Derek Thompson wrote a column for *The Atlantic*, "Why Oklahoma City Could Represent the Future of America."

Could it be? Perhaps. There's no question that the experiment worked and that Ed's core team contributed significantly to the city's rebirth. The six members of the team mobilized the assets in their networks (more about this later) to power Oklahoma City's transformation. By relentlessly focusing on collaborations to leverage private investment, the team led by example. The lesson Ed took away from Oklahoma City was clear: an entirely new strategy process needs to be designed for open, loosely connected networks. Modifications in traditional strategic planning simply do not work.

Throughout the 1990s, Ed continued to experiment. In a large-scale set of experiments over six years, he applied this new approach to distressed rural communities in Kentucky. Here, the problem was different. J.R. Wilhite, then-head of the Kentucky Cabinet for Economic Development, wanted to develop collaborative investments in these distressed communities, but he did not have the resources to invest in an extensive strategic planning process for each community. To meet the challenge, Ed built on the lessons of Oklahoma City and designed an agile strategy process that involved a series of two-day strategy workshops with community leaders in distressed counties. First, Ed worked with J.R. to assemble a core team of economic development professionals from outside the community. Then, during the first day in the county, the team fanned out and conducted a series of one-on-one interviews. The team then came back together in the afternoon to distill what they had learned. In the evening, Ed took these insights and drafted a "strategic action plan," which the team then presented to the community on the second day. Through these discussions, they made quick modifications. Once everyone was in agreement, the Cabinet charged the community leaders with the responsibility for implementing the strategic action plan and scheduled a six-month checkup to measure progress. This new approach to strategy proved to be remarkably successful: 18 of the 23 distressed counties made measurable progress.

A third early experiment took place in Charleston, South Carolina in 2001 with the launch of the Charleston Digital Corridor. Using lessons from both Oklahoma City and Kentucky, Ed helped Ernest Andrade formulate the early strategy for the Corridor. Ernest, a city employee, thought that Charleston was not doing enough to support high-tech, high-growth companies. He wanted to design the Charleston Digital Corridor as a new type of accelerator. There was only one problem: Ernest did not have many resources. Although he had strong support from the mayor, he began with (literally) only a logo. Despite these modest beginnings, Ernest was able to build a vibrant ecosystem by following the principles of Strategic Doing. Relentlessly building new collaborations and focusing on "doing the do-able," Ernest has been able to build a globally recognized high-technology ecosystem in Charleston.

By 2005, his experiences had convinced Ed that a new approach to strategy was possible, and he moved to Purdue University to continue to mature these ideas. There, he met Scott Hutcheson and the two of them went to work on a project that Scott had landed for the university. Purdue had received a $15 million three-year grant from the US Department of Labor to experiment with innovations in the workforce development systems in the Indiana counties around the university. The region was one of 13 regions funded across the United States. Workforce development is exceptionally complex: a number of different actors are involved, including workforce development boards, community colleges, four-year institutions, high schools, and, of course, employers, current employees, and students just entering the workforce. Using the skills of Strategic Doing, Scott and Ed assembled a core team of six people and began to build a network of collaborations with the region.

They treated their investment funds much like a venture capitalist. They invested in collaborations that had good prospects for being replicable, scalable, and sustainable, using a phased investment process to nurture successful collaborations. When the federal government tallied the results from all the regions, Purdue's approach generated returns far in excess of the investment made (we'll describe more about this initiative in Chapter 7).

OUR CURRENT WORK

These experiences were the beginning of Strategic Doing. Since then, our work has accelerated and we've worked with companies, groups, and organizations in many areas of the country – a number of which you'll read more about later in the book. We've developed a set of executive education offerings, taught by a team of Strategic Doing practitioners from around the country, using an interactive, simulation-based approach. And we've begun teaching undergraduate and graduate students at Purdue how to collaborate. While teachers of all levels regularly ask their students to work in groups, most students have never learned how to do so effectively – nor do their instructors really know how to teach these skills.

Our work is not limited to the United States. Beginning in 2014, organizations in Australia, Canada, Mexico, and Europe began connecting with us, and we began traveling abroad to share the lessons we are learning about how to design and guide complex collaboration. We've been excited to see that although the national or cultural context does make a difference in how the conversations are shaped, the basic skills needed for effective collaboration across networks are the same. Meanwhile, the demand for new ways of working together keeps growing. Over 3,000 participants from 145 countries signed up for our first Massive Open Online Courses (MOOCs) last year.

As our work in the United States and around the world began to accelerate, we realized that we needed a model to scale the expansion of this discipline. We have chosen to expand the discipline by forming an international network of colleges and universities committed to using and teaching these new skills. Following the emerging models of open source development, we have formed a nonprofit institute to manage a growing network of higher education institutions equipped to teach this new discipline. Affiliate colleges and universities agree to work through the Strategic Doing Institute to share what they are learning, exchange curricula, and improve the discipline.

Purdue is the founding member of the network, because the university sees this kind of work as part of its mission as a *land grant* institution. As the United States was industrializing in the nineteenth century, Congress saw the need to create a new kind of higher education institution. Up until the 1860s, higher education in the United States was dominated by private universities affiliated with different religious denominations (think Harvard, Yale, Princeton). The Morrill Act of 1862, signed by President Lincoln, opened the door to something different. The act provided grants of land to states that were willing to establish and endow new higher education institutions. States could take the federal land grant, sell the land, and create an endowment to launch a new university. But there were strings attached: Congress directed that the institutions established under the Morrill Act focus on teaching practical disciplines in agriculture, engineering, science, and military science. In other words, land grant universities are focused on developing new knowledge and translating this knowledge into practical applications. It's no surprise, when you understand this history, that Purdue has incubated the development of Strategic Doing for over a decade.

YOUR GUIDES FOR THIS BOOK

Five members of the Strategic Doing core team are authors of this book. Each of us is both a practitioner of Strategic Doing and a teacher, helping others to master the skills we describe here. Together, we will guide you to understand these new skills and how you can apply them both individually and in your teams. Let us give you a little background on us, your guides.

Ed Morrison is director of the Purdue Agile Strategy Lab. Ed started his career in Washington, DC, where he was legislative assistant to an Ohio congressman, staff attorney in the Office of Policy Planning for the Federal Trade Commission, and a staff member for the Senate Democratic Policy Committee, where he focused on legislation involving tax, trade, and competitiveness. After leaving Washington, he joined a corporate strategy consulting firm, where he conducted strategy studies for large companies like Ford, Volvo, and General Electric. After his work as a corporate strategy consultant, Ed consulted with communities and regions on how to tackle the complex challenges of building a prosperous economy in an era of globalization. Frustrated with existing approaches to these issues, more than 25 years ago he began working on a new methodology– the process that has grown into Strategic Doing. In 2005, Ed moved to Purdue University to incubate the discipline and teach it to others.

Scott Hutcheson is associate director of the Purdue Agile Strategy Lab and a faculty member in the School of Engineering Technology at Purdue. A master teacher, Scott has led moving Strategic Doing into the classroom and also spearheads a growing research portfolio. He teaches both undergraduate and graduate level courses in agile strategy and collaborative leadership. Scott began his career at Purdue as an engagement professional exploring how to build complex collaborations between the university and the communities it serves, and was part of the original team that launched the Purdue Center for Regional Development. He has worked extensively in nonprofit, university, and business settings. Prior to coming to Purdue, Scott held positions at the United Way of Central Indiana and American Airlines.

Liz Nilsen is senior program director at the Purdue Agile Strategy Lab. She guides the growth of Strategic Doing, managing the network of affiliate colleges and universities that are teaching Strategic Doing in undergraduate, graduate, and executive education programs. She also leads the development of new offerings and oversees the training sequence we use with faculty and Strategic Doing practitioners worldwide. She has led the lab's work in the transformation of engineering education, as well as our work with NASA. Prior to coming to Purdue, Liz was part of an initiative to embed innovation and entrepreneurship in undergraduate engineering education. Under Liz's guidance, 50 university teams from around the United States learned Strategic Doing and used the discipline to launch more than 500 collaborative efforts in under three years (you'll read more about this project later on). Liz has an extensive higher education background and began her career in nonprofit management.

Janyce Fadden is director of strategic engagement at the University of North Alabama. Janyce is a principal architect of Shoals Shift, a multifaceted innovation initiative in Alabama's Muscle Shoals region. This initiative, based on Strategic Doing, is developing a dynamic entrepreneurial ecosystem in a region not traditionally associated with innovation beyond the music industry. Prior to coming to the University of North Alabama, Janyce led the Rockford (Illinois) Area Economic Development Council for nearly a decade. In that position, she guided the development of a series of strategic initiatives to build the region's aerospace cluster, its workforce and talent pipeline, and its entrepreneurship support networks. Janyce also has an extensive private sector background: she has served as a marketing director at

Honeywell; as the president of Leeds and Northrup, a division of General Signal; and as vice president and general manager at two divisions within Danaher Corporation.

Nancy Franklin leads Franklin Solutions, a consulting firm that guides leaders in universities, government agencies, and community organizations in strategic initiatives, innovation, and change initiatives. Nancy is a national leader in university engagement initiatives in which universities build complex collaborations with the communities they serve. She previously led strategic initiatives at Penn State, Virginia Tech, and Indiana State University. Nancy uses Strategic Doing to work across organizational boundaries to develop shared goals and to execute effective strategies. She has deployed Strategic Doing in numerous settings, including regional development, higher education–community partnerships, and corporate supply chain innovation.

Books written by more than one person face the unique challenge of deciding what wording to use when describing experiences by members of the team. In this book, we usually just use the pronoun "we," although in a few cases (including the case studies, all of which describe initiatives in which one or more of us has been directly involved) we'll identify exactly which of us was involved.

WHY THIS BOOK?

Fads come and go. Whether it is the latest management model or the newest leadership book, we have all seen new ideas that end up being nothing more than a flash in the pan. As we hope we've convinced you by now, the practitioners and researchers committed to Strategic Doing are different. We are committed to a new discipline of strategy specifically designed for open, loosely connected networks. We are committed to continuously improving this discipline through rigorous testing and evaluation. Finally, we are committed to transformation. The economic, social, and political institutions at the core of our developed economies desperately need an overhaul. It's been clear for a long time that designing these transformations would require us to collaborate. Yet for most people, "collaborate" is just a word used to dress up the usual series of endless and ineffective meetings. It doesn't have to be that way.

To unpack these ideas, the book is arranged in three sections:

You Are Here: Before introducing the skills, it's important to understand the nature of our challenges, how the world has fundamentally changed and the implications for strategy, and the changes we ourselves need to make. We know that some of you will skip right to the skills chapters, but we think you'll get much more out of them if you understand *why* the approach has to be different than traditional methodologies.

The Ten Skills of Agile Leadership: In a set of chapters, we'll unpack each of the ten skills. In addition, we'll provide some guidance about how you might start using the skill, and also illustrate how that skill was critical in a particular situation in a case study (while there are people using these skills all over the world, each of the case studies is drawn from a situation in which one of us was directly involved). Even if your challenge or organization is different from the one we describe, we hope the example will help you see how the skill can be adapted to specific scenarios.

Ten Skills. Got It. Now What? We don't want to just leave you with a list of ten "to-do's." In this closing section, we'll show you how the skills can be combined to amplify their effectiveness and, more generally, how to use the skills in different kinds of contexts.

In this book, we aim to show you that collaboration — and the human potential it unleashes — emerges from a portfolio of skills that can be widely distributed within a team of individuals. Each person committed to a collaboration can understand and practice these skills. At the same time, we can also recognize that none of us will be equally good at all the skills. As a collaboration moves through a predictable cycle from idea generation to implementation and evaluation, members of the team bring different skills to bear. The virtues of a team emerge as leadership is passed around based on each individual's strengths. The purpose of this book is to help you recognize these skills and where your strengths lie (as well as your limitations). We want you to become a more effective leader *and* team participant.

OUR CREDO

For over 10 years, a small group of practitioners we call the core team has come together three to four times a year to share what we've learned and to explore how to improve the discipline. Indeed, we practice Strategic Doing *on* Strategic Doing. At one of these meetings, we decided to dig a little deeper. We drafted a credo (which means "I believe" in Latin) as a simple statement of what motivates us to do this work.

We want to introduce this credo to you early, so you can understand the depth of commitment that drew us to writing this book. We believe that the obligations expressed in this credo can extend to all individuals in our society and to government, business, and nonprofit organizations:

- We believe we have a responsibility to build a prosperous, sustainable future for ourselves and future generations.
- No individual, organization, or place can build that future alone.
- Open, honest, focused, and caring collaboration among diverse participants is the path to accomplishing clear, valuable, shared outcomes.
- We believe in doing, not just talking – and in behavior in alignment with our beliefs.

For us the credo is a statement of shared values that can help us overcome the silos that weaken our creativity. It is a statement of our inescapable interdependence.

POSTSCRIPT

As you read about the different skills, some of you may be wondering about whether there is underlying research supporting our work. Strategic Doing emerged from fieldwork conducted with hundreds of groups and thousands of participants over 25 years. As we distilled the discipline around ten core skills of complex collaboration, the academics among us began searching the literature to understand why these skills are so effective. We learned that existing academic research supports the development of each of these ten skills, but also that, until now, no one had put all the puzzle pieces together. It's not surprising, because the academic research is not centralized in any one discipline but instead spans a number of fields, including cognitive psychology, strategic management, and behavioral economics. We'll refer to some of this research in the book, although it is written for practitioners rather than academics. If you'd like to refer to a particular source yourself for a fuller understanding, a full citation can be found in the "Learn More" section that's at the end of the book and is arranged by chapter.

NOTE

1. "Strategic Doing" is a registered trademark. It would be tiresome indeed to keep reminding readers of this fact by following the phrase with "TM" throughout the book, so we point it out at the outset here for the usual legal reasons but have otherwise omitted it.

Chapter 1

YOU ARE HERE

THE CHALLENGES WE FACE

Let's start with a thought experiment. Assume you and your partner are parents of two teenage children, one boy and one girl. You have two weeks in the summer to take a vacation. How do you plan it? There are two ways you could make the decision. Under Option A, you and your partner simply decide that you're going to the Grand Canyon for two weeks and that your children have no say in the matter. You've made your decision by carefully analyzing the facts about travel times and budgets. All that's left is to declare your intention and go.

Option B might be to convene a discussion with your family to explore options. Your son might want to go to Charlottesville, Virginia and Washington, DC because he's interested in learning more about Thomas Jefferson. Your daughter, on the other hand, has an interest in genealogy, and she wants to go to Cincinnati to visit her grandmother and learn more about the origins of your family. Your partner suggests a trip to Seattle, because none of you have ever gone to the Pacific Northwest. You would prefer a trip to Boston and Maine, where you could, among other things, introduce the family to the joys of eating a lobster. With all these options, how do you decide? Chances are, you'd convene a family conversation, or maybe several, to see if you could come up with a plan that is at least acceptable to everyone.

Nobel Prize winner Herbert Simon called this second approach *sat isficing*, a combination of the verbs "to satisfy" and "to suffice." It means searching through available options and figuring out a solution that meets a minimum threshold of acceptability, a vacation that is "good enough" to satisfy everyone. Contrast this approach to Option A, which is more of a command-and-control decision with one decision maker, presumably in possession of all the relevant facts, making a rational decision.

Option B requires deeper conversations, and an embrace of ambiguity – and that's the point. Planning a family vacation is a complex project with no single, simple, rational answer. Each of us has a different idea of the ideal vacation. We have many options of what we could do. There is no way to put all of these factors into some equation and come up with an optimal answer. Instead, we learn to muddle through to a satisfactory solution.

3

As our example of a family vacation shows, most of us have some experience working with complex problems. We have some direct experience with both satisficing and muddling through. They are useful concepts when relatively few people are involved. But what happens when dozens or hundreds of people are involved? That's real complexity, and most of us don't have an approach to cope with it.

In essence, that's the problem we faced in Oklahoma City in the early 1990s: How do we make decisions about priorities with a lot of people involved if nobody can tell anyone else what to do? How do we make sensible choices? If no one person (such as the mayor) or no one organization (such as the Chamber of Commerce) can pull Oklahoma City out of its economic tailspin, what should we do?

Even today, companies, organizations, and communities facing complex challenges still try to opt for Option A. They try to find a rational answer by analyzing data – *lots of data*. Once an ostensibly rational answer is determined by a small group (to be fair, they've usually also included some way for a larger number of people to communicate their own preferences), they announce it and expect everyone else to follow. This is part of the traditional approach to *strategic planning*. But as many of those who have sat on a strategic planning committee will attest, this approach is increasingly unworkable (we'll explain why later in this chapter).

Companies face complexity every day. How do they make their organizations more agile? Rapid changes in consumer demand, technologies, regulations, and competition put a premium on the ability to respond and adapt quickly. Yet, most companies are caught in rigidity. Most are structured around functions, like marketing and finance; yet, innovation – the life force of any business – is not housed within any of these functions. Job descriptions may provide clarity to employees, but they also draw a fence around employee contributions to new ideas. Quality systems provide stability to existing products, but they do not encourage the experimental mindsets needed to discover "what's next." Fear and risk aversion too often stifle new thinking. Instead of embracing new ideas, many companies have an immune system that is triggered to kill them. As one top manager in a Fortune 100 company asked us, "How do I make 10,000 employees more innovative?" A complex challenge, indeed.

The challenges faced by nonprofit organizations are no less daunting. As income disparities increase, the demands for social services accelerate, but resources are not keeping up. What's the result? Nonprofit managers are faced with increased competition for funding, while funders (trying to find a coherent way to allocate resources) demand ever more in the way of metrics and accountability. Without some way to manage this complexity, these factors set the stage for personal and professional burnout. University administrators are in a similar bind. The role of the university in the knowledge economy is rapidly shifting as declining public funding, new learning technologies, and continuously shifting market demands place different pressures on higher education institutions.

Closer to home, think of some of the complexities that our communities face. Our friends in Flint confront the collapse of both public safety (in the form of a severely weakened police department) and public health (the collapse of the city's water system). Across the United States, drug addiction, principally opioids, is killing about 65,000 Americans a year (about 180 people a day), with no community untouched. The epidemic of gun violence kills about half the number of people as drug overdoses, but the numbers are still staggering: about 38,000 Americans die from gun-related injury each year (one third from homicides, two thirds from suicides).

Now step back and think as a global citizen. Climate change is accelerating. Global population is due to increase to 9.8 billion people by 2040. Energy demand will increase more than 50% by 2040. We need a 60% increase in food production by 2050, if global population grows as is currently forecast. We must rapidly answer some compelling questions:

- How can we assure people access to clean water without conflicts?
- How can our energy and food demands be met?
- How do we reduce the threats of terrorism and the use of weapons of mass destruction?
- How can we address climate change?

All of these challenges are daunting in large part because they are embedded in *complex adaptive systems*. A complex system is a system in which many independent components (or "agents") interact with one another. As they do, they learn or adapt in response to their interactions. Examples of complex systems range from individual cells to cities, ecosystems, our climate and, indeed, our universe. These systems are difficult to model, because they have so many different agents creating a mind-boggling array of interactions. Although scientists have been studying complex systems for a long time, it was not until the establishment of the Santa Fe Institute in 1984 that the study of complex systems became firmly established as an independent field of research. The Institute's scholars provided the intellectual frameworks for practitioners to explore complex collaboration in a practical way.

The fact is that we are becoming overwhelmed by challenges that reside in these kinds of complex systems, but many of us are approaching the challenges with disciplines and mind-sets developed decades ago. Is it any wonder that our trust and confidence in institutions generally – business, government agencies, nonprofit organizations, higher education, and faith-based organizations – has eroded?

Some years ago, Horst Rittel and Melvin Webber wrote a paper describing the concept of "wicked problems." These are problems that are difficult or impossible to solve because our information is incomplete or contradictory. What's more, conditions are continuously changing. Because of the interdependencies within the complex systems that give rise to wicked problems, an effort to solve one problem can give rise to others. We can quickly create "unintended consequences." There is no simple solution to a wicked problem. Proposed solutions are neither wholly right nor completely wrong, and every wicked problem is unique.

The point is simply this: in our families, organizations, and communities we are increasingly confronted with these complex, "wicked" problems. Yet we have not advanced our thinking or, until now, developed new protocols or approaches to addressing these complex problems. We know that no single organization or individual can solve a complex problem. Indeed, every solution we develop is temporary – when conditions inevitably change, we will have to adjust.

WHAT, EXACTLY, HAS CHANGED?

The challenges we describe earlier are critical, but if we don't understand the fundamental shifting dynamic in our world, we will miss the key to addressing them. There is something else at work that is easily overlooked, or at least is so much a part of our current reality that we have ceased to notice it.

It wasn't that long ago that nearly everyone in the world lived their lives in small groups of extended families – many on farms, others in what today we would call "small businesses." There was a predictable rhythm to life, often structured around the seasons, and each family would – for the most part – make their own decisions about which activities needed to be done and when, to ensure the well-being of the whole.

In the middle of the 1800s, that began to change, particularly in the West. New machines made it possible to produce things people needed or wanted – cloth, farm equipment, processed food – much faster than had ever been done before. Companies formed around these new technologies and began to draw people into cities for work to create these new goods. This "industrial revolution" opened new possibilities – young people could learn a set of skills, work their way up, and live a life very different from what would have been possible on the farm.

But as with most big transitions, there was a trade-off. These new jobs didn't come with the same freedom to organize one's own days, weeks, and months. There was a supervisor to answer to. And soon, those supervisors were listening to a new kind of expert, a "management consultant" who talked about "efficiencies" and timed each part of a job, finding ways to shave off even hundredths of a second from each component of a task, in order to maximize profits.

Each worker had a supervisor, who was also overseen by a supervisor, and there was *another* supervisor after that. This structure – the *hierarchy* – came to characterize the world of work (and many other spheres as well). There were charts that explained exactly who could tell which people what to do, and you could get a pretty good idea of how things worked in the company by looking at one of these new "organization charts."

Hierarchies weren't just for factories. The movie industry in the first half of the twentieth century is a good example of how a hierarchy functioned. When a studio decided to make a movie, it called on a full complement of people to make the film a reality. Directors, producers, set builders, food services – even the actors themselves and the managers of many of the theaters – all were employed by the studio and were told exactly what they could and could not do.

The hierarchy allowed the studios to control every aspect of the film-making process.[1] For example, the 1935 movie *David Copperfield* was made with about 70 people – nearly all of them employed by MGM, in a structure much like the one shown in Figure 1.1. The system was so productive, in fact, that the studios released about 700 films *every year* in the 1920s.

You can see that the hierarchy had definite advantages. The key to productivity was controlling the lines of communication, and the "org chart" described those lines in great detail.

David Copperfield probably wouldn't draw many people to the theater these days. What happened?

In a word – television. Suddenly people didn't need to go to the theater to be entertained; the box in their living room could deliver stories to them every night. If movies were going to survive, they would need to be different to draw audiences in: new technologies, special effects, filming in exotic locations. And television wasn't the end of the change for the movie industry, although it's taken several decades to see the transition clearly. Now, it's not just the box in your house, it's the tablet you take on the plane and the tiny screen in your pocket (and undoubtedly there will be more vehicles for delivering good stories to us in the future). Network TV, cable, streaming services, and even individuals with just a video camera and a YouTube account – all can deliver a captivating tale to a community of interested viewers.

Movies are still with us, but the studios have had to change the way they do business in a very significant way to compete for our attention. Take a fairly recent example, *The Hobbit*. Like *David Copperfield*, the *Hobbit* franchise is also an MGM product, but as with most films today, when you watch one of the films that make up the franchise, you see the names of several companies in the opening credits: in this case, three other production companies. Each is playing a different role

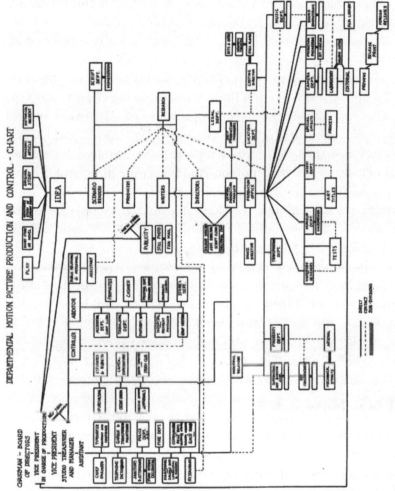

Figure 1.1 Twentieth Century Fox Film Corporation, 1940s organization chart.
Source: Twentieth Century Fox, unpublished document, n.d.

in getting J.R.R. Tolkien's story to the big screen. Ian McKellen and Martin Freeman, two of the stars, can work for whatever studio they would like and can dictate the terms of their work. Some companies working on the films don't show up in the opening montage, but you can spot more than 60 of them in the tiny credits at the end. The budget for *The Hobbit* was about $745 million, and that paid for thousands of people (more than 2,700 just on the first film) to work on the films over seven years – but very few of them were actually employed by MGM itself.

It would take a very large piece of paper indeed to draw the org chart for *The Hobbit* – and it wouldn't much resemble the older example's. Rather than hierarchies, the movie industry is now organized around networks. For each film, the studio assembles the partners, actors, and contractors it needs for that particular project. Some may have worked together before, others may be new. And when the film "wraps," that particular constellation of people and organizations will never again work together. Does it work? Decide for yourself: in the case of the *Hobbit* films, the investment of $745 million brought in more than $3 billion in revenue – a pretty good return.

Just as hierarchies weren't limited to factories, networks aren't limited to the movie industry. They are all around us and have become the primary organizing structure behind most of the goods we buy, the services we use, and the places we work, live, and play. Very few things in our complex world can be accomplished by a single individual or company working in isolation.

What Is a Network?

Although the *Hobbit* example sketches out the general contours of a network in action, we want to be a bit more precise about what a network is. A network (see Figure 1.2 for a visual depiction) has several important characteristics:

- It forms around a set of assets, or resources. These assets might take many forms: a physical location, a particular technology, even an intangible set of ideas that people hold in common. We often call this set of assets the *hub* of the network.

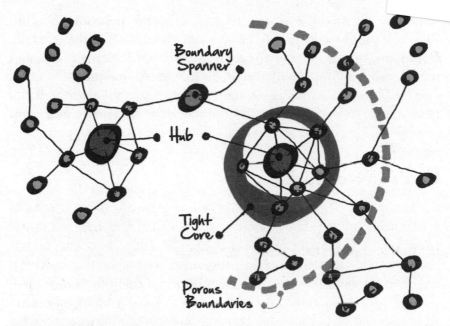

Figure 1.2   Network structure.
Source: Strategic Doing Institute.

- There is usually a set of people who are particularly closely related to the hub. They may be the people who formed the initial network. Communication is easiest within this *core*, particularly if they are geographically in the same location.
- There are other people who are more loosely connected. They may not even be connected to the hub directly, but rather connected through someone else. It's challenging to get a message to all of these people, particularly those on the periphery.
- The network is never static. There may be people who start off in the core but then become less connected, while there may be other people who become more deeply involved over time. The boundary dividing who is "in" and who is "out" of the network is a porous one.
- There is no "top" or "bottom" to a network. There is no one individual or entity that can give directions for the members to carry out.

Often, a network exists in relation to other networks, because there are people who are part of both networks. We call these people "boundary spanners." These other networks may have some interests in common in some circumstances, but there are probably other circumstances in which their interests aren't so well-aligned. If the networks are to work together in some way, they will have to find a way to align their resources so that their efforts are not at cross-purposes.

Kinds of Networks

There are several different kinds of networks, each with a particular function. Some are *advocacy networks*, made up of people who work to advance a particular cause or idea. Members don't necessarily know each other, but all are part of the network because of its mission. *Learning networks*, such as professional associations, form because a group of people wants to increase their knowledge or skills in a particular area. At least some of the members usually know one another reasonably well. These kinds of networks have value in accelerating an individual's learning, but what we are really after is an *innovating network*. These networks are composed of people who have joined forces to *create new value together*. They are a bit like the children's story *Stone Soup*, in which a clever cook starts by putting a stone in a large pot of water and invites her neighbors to add whatever they have. One brings a carrot, another tosses in a potato, a third has a leftover bone with a bit of meat still on it. By the story's end, of course, the pot is full of delicious soup for all to share. In an innovating network, each person brings their own resources to the network, and together they create something that is more than the sum of its parts.

An interesting example of an innovating network is the group of companies that came together to create what we think of as the product of a single company – the iPod. While Apple was certainly at the center of the network, dozens of other companies had a hand in its birth, including hardware parts manufacturers, music distributors, accessory designers, and more (a graphic of this network, from one of the earlier iPods, is shown in Figure 1.3). Apple founder Steve Jobs may have been a genius, but part of his particular legerdemain was in assembling the right collection of partners to bring the iPod to market.

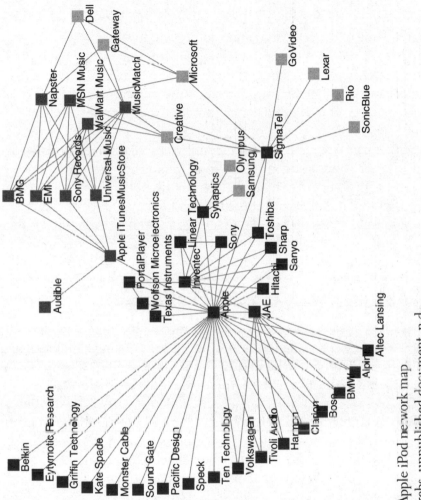

Figure 1.3 Apple iPod network map
Source: Valdis Krebs, unpublished document, n.d.

13

The Habitat of Networks

Networks are found in nearly every conceivable setting. Some networks, as in the iPod or *Hobbit* examples, bring together separate companies for a particular joint venture. On a much larger scale, the European Union is a network of countries, or more accurately, their governments. Nonprofit organizations often join forces to work on a shared issue of concern or to apply for a grant together.

These examples illustrate networks that cross organizational boundaries. Not all networks do so – there are also networks within single organizations. Different units of a company may form an internal network because of a particular new product that requires each of the units' capabilities.

Sometimes what looks like a hierarchy is actually a network in disguise. There may be an organizational chart, but the reality on the ground is that people have a great deal of discretion in whether to go along with what the people at the top want to happen. Universities are one example of this phenomenon – the tradition of tenure means that many individual faculty members can (for the most part) decide if and how they will support the president's latest set of "strategic priorities."

Hierarchies, Networks, and Strategy

These two distinct organizational structures – the hierarchy and the network – have very different implications for thinking about strategy. In a hierarchy, the challenge is to communicate information about what to do *down*, and to get information about the results *up*.

In a network, on the other hand, the challenge is to get the members' resources and efforts *aligned* toward a chosen objective. The capacity to execute a particular strategy across the network may be very large, but only if the network's assets can be efficiently marshaled.

This is a key difference – and necessitates thinking about "doing" strategy very differently. A network is itself a complex system, which is often operating within a larger complex system – be it an industry environment, a regional ecosystem, higher education, or the web of influences that are part of a specific social challenge.

However, our primary approach to strategy – strategic planning – hasn't yet adapted to this enormous transition. In fact, we believe it cannot (at least as we have traditionally thought of the approach[2]). Strategic planning has its roots in World War II, as military leaders learned how to apply systems thinking to complex problems, like the invasion of Normandy on D-Day. The approach then found its way into corporations in the postwar period. In the 1960s, the rational, linear school of strategic planning took root in business schools. In other words, it was designed in and for an age in which the hierarchy was the dominant organizational paradigm.

As was the case with the movie industry, strategic planning works well when two conditions are met. First, the environment must be visible and stable. It doesn't change much. Second, there needs to be a command-and-control structure in place to facilitate communication. A small group of leaders can be sure that everyone else will follow their direction. In other words, a small group of people at the top of the organization is thinking, and the rest of the organization does the doing.

Most of the world does not work like that anymore, which is one of the main reasons why strategic planning is so often ineffective. Instead the world is increasingly dominated – both inside and outside our organizations – by *open, loosely connected networks*. That is, the networks are more or less voluntary, as people (or organizations) join together not because they are all part of a single hierarchy, but because they have a particular task to complete which can best be done by all of them working together. Both the Apple and *Hobbit* examples describe just such networks.

THE S-CURVE

A powerful way to conceptualize an alternative to traditional strategy thinking is to consider the idea of a life cycle. We use a visual representation of a life cycle: the S-Curve. S-Curves help us understand what is happening at various points in the cycle – or, to put it more broadly, in any change process. You can see two of these curves in Figure 1.4.

S-Curves explain many different kinds of change – how new technologies enter the market and grow, how companies or organizations behave over the course of years or decades, and even many biological processes, such as human development. In all of these scenarios, events follow a similar progression (look at a single S-Curve to follow

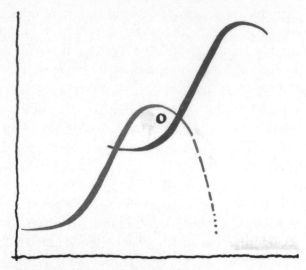

Figure 1.4   S-Curves.
Source: Strategic Doing Institute.

the sequence). At the beginning, things happen slowly. Only a few people buy the new gadget, the business starts with one person in their home office, a baby enters the world as a helpless and dependent soul. Next, there is a period of rapid growth: the new device "goes viral," the new business has to move into a dedicated facility and hire employees, the baby grows into a child and learns to walk, talk, and make its own decisions. Eventually, the growth slows and there is a period in which things seem to have reached a plateau: most people have a GPS in their car, the business has a solid core of customers coming back on a regular basis, the young adult has a career and has settled into a community with his or her own family and friends.

If we keep looking forward, we'll see the final part of the S-Curve, in which there is a decline: the smartphone makes the separate GPS device obsolete, the small business can't keep up with online shopping, and the older adult needs to move into an assisted living facility.

There are three important insights S-Curves provide:

1. Change is constant and dynamic.
2. Nothing lasts forever under its initial momentum.
3. Success contains the seeds of its own destruction.

If you're introducing a technology or other innovation it's particularly important to understand the S-Curve. Why? If your organization is approaching the plateau phase, you want to know that, so you can take action to avoid the decline phase, as the curve starts to go down. The best possible scenario would be that you would enjoy the growth in the middle part of the S-Curve and then, before the market declines, you would begin selling whatever new technology is coming along. As Figure 1.4 shows, that new technology has its own S-Curve. You want to hop from the current S-Curve to an earl(ier) point on a new one. The same principle holds true in most fields and industries, although despite many efforts (consider cryogenics) we haven't yet figured out a way for aging adults to hop into new bodies ... yet!

Our way of approaching strategy, then, needs to focus on this challenge: How do we take resources from our past and current successes (be they technologies, skills, people, and so on) and repurpose them so that we can successfully compete in new circumstances?

This is not an inconsequential challenge – moving from one S-Curve to another inevitably means that at some point you are *between* curves – and that can feel quite risky and exposed, like the trapeze performer who has to let go of one bar before grasping the next one. This is true no matter what the setting. For businesses, it means investing precious capital in R&D toward the "next thing." For many regions, it means letting go of the idea that recruiting a new large company, just like the one that closed, is the key to returning to the "good old days." Educational institutions at every level have to confront the fact that our children and grandchildren will need a new set of skills to succeed and courses, credentials, and classrooms may need to change significantly.

However, to stay where you are means that inevitably – at some point – you will be on the downward slope of the curve. Far better, then, to figure out how to navigate this new world and learn the skills of strategy in networks.

THE CHANGES WE NEED TO MAKE

What does it mean to navigate shifting circumstances in this way? Before taking on challenges "out there" in the world, each of us needs to grapple with a more personal transformation. To effectively use the tools of strategy in a networked world, we need to change three things:

1. We need to think differently.
2. We need to behave differently.
3. We need to "do" differently (this is different than behaving differently, as we'll see).

Thinking Differently

First, we need to change the way we think about strategy. Let's start with a not-so-simple question: What is strategy, anyhow?

The word strategy comes from the Greek word *straegia*, which literally means "generalship." The first understanding of strategy, then, was military. What did a general do? In war, he was responsible for the decisions about the number and location of troops to be deployed in order to fight for maximum advantage. That decision then triggered a host of smaller decisions about transportation, timing, weapons or other supplies, and so forth.

Stepping back, we could frame the general's role as asking two questions: Where are we going? and How are we going to get there? With this definition, think about the strategic plans you've recently read or been a part of developing. Many don't answer one or both of these questions. Many reflect a great deal of thinking about competitive environment, vision, and so on without getting down to the activities that would be involved in reaching those goals. Others have a laundry list of things to do, timelines, and project charts without a coherent understanding of how these fit into a bigger picture based on the needs of the community, organization, or market. Without both of these pieces, we really can't say that a plan describes a strategy – although there may have been a lot of good thinking that went into developing the plan.

Since we just finished describing how the world has changed, you may be asking whether an ancient Greek definition even makes sense anymore. The answer is yes – Where are we going? and How will we get there? are just a broader restatement of the general's challenge. However, there is a caveat: while the Greek general no doubt made most strategic decisions on his own, in a complex environment characterized by networks, it's simply not possible for one individual to develop effective strategy. Strategy has to be a team effort, and the complex the environment, the larger the group – the network – that will need to be engaged. But the essentials remain the same: the network will need to make key decisions about where they are going and how they intend to get there.

The size of a network does reflect its capacity to some extent. More critical, however, are the number of connections in the network. Consider the inventor of the first telephone, Alexander Graham Bell – if he had built only one phone, it would have been worthless. Two phones would have been an improvement, but obviously still far short of the invention's potential. With just five phones, 10 different connections were possible, and so on.[3] However, your immediate network doesn't need to be huge – remember that every network is also linked to other networks through boundary spanners. Taking advantage of this capacity so that it's not just a hypothetical potential for impact requires some kind of protocol for working together.

The word we often use for working together is *collaboration*. In fact, if there were a contest for a term that suffers most from overuse, collaboration would be a leading candidate. This is true in corporate organizations as well as nonprofit and civic environments, in which funders often require some level of collaboration.

True collaboration is at one end of a continuum of joint efforts. When people come together, they usually start by just exchanging information about who they are and what they do – we often call this *networking*. A bit more involved is *coordinating*. We alter our activities to some extent; for example, civic groups may decide to schedule their fundraising events so that they don't fall on the same weekend. Still further along the continuum is *cooperating*. When we cooperate, we agree to share some resources with one another. Employees in a small business may decide to cooperate by arranging to cover for one another so that everyone can take an annual vacation, for example.

All of these activities are good – but they aren't collaboration (although we may claim otherwise in a presentation!). Collaboration involves linking, leveraging, and aligning resources in ways that enhance one another's capacity to create a shared outcome, a mutual benefit. It can sometimes be difficult to tell if two groups are truly collaborating. Beyond the kinds of work they are doing together, we can ask two additional questions. What is the level of trust that network members have of one another? and, conversely, are network members still holding onto their turf? In moving along the continuum toward collaboration, trust increases while turf decreases. We'll share many examples of true collaboration in the coming chapters.

For really complex challenges you'll need to pay attention to both of these drivers of performance: growing the network's size so that its capacity is larger *and* moving toward truly collaborative work. Neither of these happen overnight, but both will be crucial for addressing truly "wicked" problems.

Behaving Differently

The men that gathered in 1787 in Philadelphia had a big, complex problem on their hands. The American colonists had won the war for freedom from England, but in the years since, the new nation had sputtered, unable to find a way to effectively transition from 13 rebelling colonies to a functioning democracy. Fifty-five delegates made their way to a "constitutional convention" to see if they could find a way to organize that would provide stability and prosperity.

Their work together took four months, and resulted in the US Constitution. The document wasn't perfect (as 27 amendments since then and a Civil War amply demonstrate), but it became the template for a completely new form of government.

And yet, their work began with a curious step: establishing *rules of civility*. The rules were much the same as you might wish to establish in meetings today: don't interrupt, pay attention to the speaker, and so on. The key point is that the delegates realized that the work they were embarking upon was exceedingly complex and fraught with tension. In order to navigate the discussions ahead, they recognized before they started that they needed to decide what the ground rules should be.

We noted earlier that in genuine collaboration, trust has to be high (and turf low). Since "trust" is another of those words that can mean different things to different people, here's what we mean by trust – not so much a definition as a test for its existence: trust is established when words and actions align. Rules of civility are one important component of establishing an environment where trust can flourish.

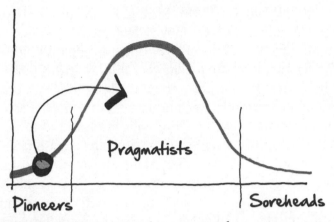

Figure 1.5 The people in a network.
Source: Strategic Doing Institute.

They allow people to make commitments to one another and then to follow through. At the Constitutional Convention, for example, a person could speak and know that others would listen to their ideas, rather than carrying on a side conversation or otherwise being disruptive. We'll come back to this idea later with Skill 1.

In addition to having rules for everyone to follow, we also need to behave differently when it comes to specific kinds of people. In any change effort, there are three kinds of people, as shown in Figure 1.5 (you may recognize the shape as a "bell curve"). At one end, there are *pioneers*, the people leading the charge and eager to change. This is usually a small group, as depicted in the graphic. Then there is a much larger group, which we can call the *pragmatists*. Pragmatists will go along with change as soon as they see that it's prudent to do so – they want to see that their time and/or reputation won't be wasted. So far, so good. But, there's a third group – those that aren't interested in joining in. They say (and keep saying) things like, "That will never work," "We've tried that before," or "What we have is good enough." We call this group the *soreheads*. Fortunately, their numbers are also few.

We are no experts in human history, but there probably has been no transformation in human civilization with no soreheads. However, too often we act as though if we just said the right thing, we could get the soreheads on our side. We let the tyranny of the few suck the energy out of our efforts. Instead, we should concentrate our efforts on getting the *pragmatists* to engage. As one university provost we know says about working with faculty: "I know there's one-third that is ready to move, and if they come along, there's another third that will join in to join the first third. And I don't worry about the last third." We don't mean that you should steamroll over the naysayers from the get-go. There are often people who look like soreheads but turn out to be pragmatists – they're just a bit slower to join up. But after a reasonable amount of effort to make sure that you understand one another, just move on. We can't let the soreheads drag us all down.

As we move forward, we need to behave differently not just when we're discussing what we might do, but when we actually begin to make decisions. We need to balance two dimensions: guidance and participation. We see these two dimensions at work all around us. When there's no guidance but lots of people involved, you get *chaos*. Even a group of ten trying to decide where to go out to dinner together is usually a frustrating experience for everyone. When there's no guidance and low participation, that's *apathy* – the meet-up that no one bothers to come to. There are also scenarios in which there's plenty of guidance but low participation – the classic *backroom deal*. In organizations, this is often cloaked in a veneer of participation (advisory committees, listening sessions, employee surveys, and the like), while at the same time everyone knows that there are a few people who will make decisions and frequently have already made up their mind.

There is another option – high participation with high guidance. Everyone's voice is heard, but the discussion is guided and has direction. This kind of decision-making generally leads to success, because there has been plenty of input, but it's also efficient – people don't feel that their time has been wasted with meetings that don't go anywhere. The skills we introduce in this book allow you to create this kind of environment.

Doing Differently

Thinking differently and behaving differently "set the table" for the third thing that needs to happen in order for companies, organizations, or communities to successfully navigate challenges – doing differently.

The ten skills in the remainder of this book break that "doing" down into specific components that are simple to understand and put into practice. They are not, however, a "one-and-done" formula. Change is constant – there is always another S-Curve, sooner or later. The doing differently needs to become a permanent way of working – a set of habits, if you will. When Ed was first casting about for a new approach in the early 1990s, he found himself in Singapore at a lunch with the chief technology officer of one of his client companies. A fellow diner, a PhD physicist, suggested that there were two new developments that would completely change how we viewed the world, and that strategy would need to change as well. The two? The internet and software design.

Unlike other forms of mass communications — radio, television — the internet is interactive. That's a big deal. The internet is our first interactive mass medium. We are still trying to figure out what that means, but with the launch of the first commercial web browser, Netscape, in 1994, it was now possible for different types of interactive connections to happen: one-to-one (email); one-to-many (e.g., YouTube), many-to-one (Kickstarter), and many-to-many (eBay). While entrepreneurs are continuing to create new business models to take advantage of this power, one fact is clear: the internet has disrupted the classical top-down hierarchy and the traditional strategic planning methodologies that supported it. The changes wrought by the internet and their application to strategy are fairly evident: every organization now operates in a global environment, and freely available information makes changes in the environment (whether competitive, social, political, etc.) visible in nearly real time.

As for software design, the model of agile software development provides a framework for thinking about strategy in this new world. New software is always produced in a team environment. The members of the team are each working on just a bit of the program at a time, and these fragments are tested immediately, and adjustments made if needed. The team meets together frequently so that they can stay on track and aligned with one another and ensure that there aren't any compatibility issues. The software is released in stages: first a 0.9 or "beta" to help shake out the bugs, and then a version 1.0, to be followed by 1.1, then 1.2, and so on. At some point, the company decides a whole new set of features is needed – version 2.0, perhaps. From the user perspective, our experience has also changed, very much for the better. At the beginning of the "personal computer" age, you bought a program in a box with a version number, and then you waited several years for the new release, which also came in a box. Once most people had internet access, companies began issuing "patches" that could be downloaded periodically to fix major issues. Today, these improvements are available much more frequently and are often automatically installed – if we're even using software that is "ours" rather than hosted in the cloud.

Additionally, much software is developed in an open source environment, an entirely new approach to conduct complex work. Linus Torvalds popularized this approach when he decided to design a new operating system for computers. The story is remarkable: Torvalds, a 21-year-old computer science student in Finland, released the "beginnings" of a new computer operating system in 1991. We say beginnings because it was and is an open source operating system, with code contributed by thousands of programmers around the world. Called Linux, it now has 23.3 million lines of source code.

Both of these aspects of software development – constant experimentation, with lessons shared among a collaborative network – characterize effective strategy today. Strategy is developed and refined by implementing modest ideas and evaluating the impact, adjusting and scaling up as you go. What is critical is that the team has a process to manage this kind of ongoing effort – ways of working together that have become firmly established with practice and discipline.

*   *   *

We've now set the stage for the ten skills by introducing some of the key concepts that explain why strategy needs to be approached differently and a few of the assumptions you'll glimpse in the pages ahead. As you encounter the skills, you may think to yourself that they seem quite simplistic – and possibly, not worth the price of this book. A few observations, then: first, we may be tempted to think that in a complex world we need a complicated strategy process. Nothing could be further from the truth – when faced with complexity, the right approach is one in which there are a limited number of principles, but ones that are robust enough to allow for many possibilities and strategic shifts where necessary. Second, while the skills are simple, that's not the same thing as simplistic. They are simple, but not easy; they require practice and attention to master. Third, the real power of the skills is in combining them – perhaps not all ten at any one time, but identifying the skills most called for in a particular situation. The whole is truly more than the sum of its parts.

But enough with the preliminaries – it's time to lift the curtain.

NOTES

1. You might also recognize this structure as classic vertical integration. Here we're focusing on the hierarchy behind that integration, because the hierarchy was the defining feature of nearly every organization, not just corporate structures seeking to produce a tangible product.

2. We hear from many people that we work with, particularly management consultants, that strategic planning itself has adapted to these new realities. We remain somewhat skeptical. We do know of cases in which companies, organizations, or regions have in fact used a process that was still called strategic planning but that was much better-suited to the network age. Far too often, however, the approach has been only marginally tweaked – the emphasis is still on retrospective data collection, hours of meetings over many months, and detailed workplans stretching far into the future for other people to operationalize. By and large, strategic planning remains a slow, costly, rigid, and often ineffective process.

3. In 2017, there were about 238 million cellphone users in the United States – that's almost 3 quindecillion connections – that's a 3 with 16 zeros [for you math geeks, the formula is $x = n(n - 1)/2$).]. (Source: Statista.)

Chapter 2

CREATE AND MAINTAIN A SAFE SPACE FOR DEEP, FOCUSED CONVERSATION (SKILL 1)

Think about the best conversations you've ever had. These were, perhaps, conversations that led to your best friend *becoming* your best friend. Or maybe they were long talks you had during the earliest days of getting to know the person who is now the love of your life. Maybe some conversations on your short list of best conversations ever were with a business partner or a mentor. Even a chat with a wide-eyed four-year-old can be a great conversation. Agile leadership means knowing how to guide conversations. This ability begins with understanding how to create and maintain a safe space where great conversations can occur. Before delving into what it means to create and maintain safe spaces let's first be sure to understand the nature of deep, focused conversations. That will help us determine the right sort of spaces in which to have them.

DEEP CONVERSATIONS

How many conversations do you think you had this week, over the last seven days? These could be conversations with your spouse or partner, your kids, or other family members. This would also include work-related conversations – conversations with your boss, with those you supervise, your peers, partners, customers, or anyone else you encounter because of work. Don't forget all the other conversations you have, like those with the person ringing up your groceries or the neighbor you encounter while taking your dog for a walk.

What is a "deep conversation"? Although there are some definitions out there, let's use the *Roosevelt Standard* to define "deep." Eleanor Roosevelt was an American politician, diplomat, and activist. She served as First Lady of the United States longer than any other presidential spouse, from 1933 to 1945 during her husband's (Franklin D. Roosevelt) time in the White House. Among her many quotable comments is this one: Great minds discuss ideas; average minds discuss events; small minds discuss people. We'll use that as our guide for how shallow or deep our conversations are. Our most shallow of conversations are more likely to be about people, moving to somewhat more depth when discussing events, and the greatest of depths when we discuss ideas with one another. With that as your standard, where do you stand? How many of your week's conversations were discussions of *ideas*?

Of course, not every conversation needs to be a deep one. Many of the daily tasks of business and life can be accomplished with conversations that skim, appropriately, right along the surface. The discussion of what to have for dinner on a given evening need not always lead to the ideas embedded in our take-out pizza. There is, however, some evidence that we are hardwired to need and even thrive on a certain amount of deep, substantive conversation. In a study led by the University of Arizona, researchers found that higher rates of well-being were associated with spending less time alone and more time talking to others. This finding confirmed what had been found in several other studies.

In addition, however, they also found that higher rates of well-being were significantly related to participating in less small-talk conversations and more deep, substantive conversations. When they compared the unhappiest participants in the study with the happiest, they found that the happy bunch had roughly one-third as much small talk and twice as many deep, substantive conversations. The study did not attempt to explain the causal relationship behind this finding, but it raised the possibility that happiness and well-being can be raised by increasing the time spent in deep, substantive conversations. Combining this idea with our *Roosevelt Standard*, the more we discuss ideas with others, the happier and more satisfied we are likely to be.

FOCUSED CONVERSATIONS

Writing a book takes focus. Focus is hard to come by. That might have something to do with why it took us so long to get this one written. Time to focus and time to have focused conversations won't just happen. For most of us, life is just too busy. Focus requires discipline. Researchers at Carnegie Mellon's Human-Computer Interaction Lab (in partnership with the *New York Times*) think they may have an explanation as to why it's becoming increasingly difficult to make time to focus. We've known for quite some time that multitasking (what researchers sometimes call "rapid toggling between tasks") comes at a cost. Rapid toggling is a habit many of us have developed: working on a draft of a

memo, reading and responding to email, checking our s
jumping around from one task to another and back again,
space of a few minutes. This switching comes with a cognitive impact.
In our work day, many of us get only 11 minutes between each interruption and it takes an average of 25 minutes to return to the original
task after an interruption.

Imagine you are writing an important report for work. On your computer, your email program is likely running in the background and you
probably have your cellphone nearby. On average, you won't go for
more than 11 minutes before an email notification pops up on your
computer, your phone alerts you to breaking news, a text message, or
maybe you get an actual phone call. Also, a knock could come on your
office door, or if you happen to be working at home the dryer may buzz
letting you know you can put in the next load (which is currently sitting
wet in the washer). Attend to just one of these interruptions and it could
be 25 minutes before you get back to focusing fully on your report . . .
for another 11 minutes. Like deep conversations, focused conversations
won't just happen. We need to deliberately shut out potential distractions, even for just a short amount of time.

DEEP, FOCUSED GROUP CONVERSATIONS

We've established that deep, focused conversations are a rarity for most
of us. This is probably the case whether we consider one-on-one conversations and likely even more elusive when it comes to group conversations. Agile leaders who can increase the productivity of groups
and teams will be well on their way to making marked progress on
the complex, strategic challenges they are facing our organizations or
communities. Increasing the productivity of groups and teams begins
with increasing the productivity of their conversations. There are several ways we can address this.

Group Size

One of the ways to assure deep, focused group conversations is to pay
attention to the size of the group having the conversation. There is a
bit of a "Goldilocks" principle at work when it comes to optimal group

size: there is too small, too big, and just right. Perhaps you've heard of Amazon's Jeff Bezos's "two-pizza" rule for team size. He contends that if you can't feed a group with a couple of pizzas, your group is too big. It seems that Bezos's intuition is backed up by science.

In *Decide & Deliver: 5 Steps to Breakthrough Performance in your Organization*, Marcia Blenko and her coauthors contend that the ideal group size is seven and that every person beyond seven reduced the team's effectiveness by 10%, so that when a group gets to about 17 members about all they can do is to make a decision about when to take a lunch break. Others have advocated for a slightly smaller size. A 2000 study in *Psychological Sciences* finds a group of five persons as optimal. What both of these optimal numbers have in common is that five and seven are both odd numbers. An additional study, this one in *Organizational Science*, confirms that having an odd number of people in a group is better than an even number. It isn't always under our control, but when we are able to predetermine who is part of a group doing complex work together, being intentional about group size can increase the group's odds for success.

Safe Places for Conversations

With a better understanding of what a deep conversation really is, the benefits of a focused conversation, and optimal group size for doing complex strategic work, we can now turn our attention to the spaces and places where such conversations can best occur. As with group size, we don't always have the ability to determine where and when strategic conversations will happen. Whenever possible, however, it is preferable to give this some thought and to do some preplanning. In our work with the National Aeronautics and Space Administration (NASA) we had scientists coming together from several of the agency's different locations. Having a workshop on anyone's home turf would not have been the best idea. One reason is that there could be a real or perceived home field advantage with the host unit in the position to knowingly or unknowingly tilt the advantage of the collaboration toward his or her own agenda. Also, for those attending from the hosting unit, the potential for the distractions of running back to one's workstations during breaks or even sleeping in their own homes while others were far from home, would not be ideal either. Instead, we selected a location for the first gathering that was neutral and, as one of our colleagues describes it, equally inconvenient for everyone involved. In our work to bring together a global company and smaller potential partners, we chose a community college for our workshops. Why? Because we wanted to establish the idea that collaborations can most easily emerge on neutral turf.

In communities, it is especially important to pay attention to the local context when deciding where to have strategic conversations. Suppose you are bringing together a group to think about a particularly complex issue like educational attainment rates or the increasing number of people becoming addicted to opioids. The school or the health department might seem like logical places for these challenges but that may not be the case. Is the school neutral territory in a discussion about education? In our experiences working with communities, the library is often a safe space for strategic conversations about civic issues. A library has some basic rules of behavior, and usually there's no such thing as a dumb question at the library.

We've also seen great results having strategic conversations in places like children's museums. There's something about that kind of space that is conducive to the dynamics needed for strategic conversations. It could be something called the *teddy bear principle* at work: there is evidence that when adults are exposed to childhood cues they exhibit more prosocial behavior. These cues can be obvious – toys in the room, for instance. Or not quite so obvious, like using lots of colorful markers on a whiteboard instead of just black.

Safe Spaces for Conversations

Along with safe physical places, the notion of safe behavior is equally important – a safe space in which everyone can participate. Perhaps more than any other writer and researcher, Amy Edmondson of the Harvard Business School has advanced our understanding of this topic in her work on *psychological safety*. Edmondson describes psychological safety as a shared belief among members of a team or group that they are safe in taking interpersonal risks. In psychologically safe teams, team members feel accepted and respected. She offers several characteristics of psychological safety and many others have built on her work, offering insights of their own. At least one well-known company, Google, has made psychological safety a priority; it is an important factor in how they approach teamwork.

As a leader, how do you assure psychological safety in creating and maintaining safe spaces for deep focused conversations? Returning to a topic we touched on briefly in the first chapter, some great lessons can be learned from our nation's history. In her book, A *Brilliant Solution: Inventing the American Constitution*, Carol Berkin outlines how something akin to psychological safety played a foundational role in the formation of the United States.[1]

A decade after the signing of the Declaration of Independence, the fledgling nation was threatened by a tug-of-war between the states and the central government. The young nation's leaders decided to convene a Continental Congress to draft the Constitution of the United States. Expecting that these would not be easy conversations, the first order of business was to draft the rules that would govern their conversations. James Madison recorded the rules that were finally agreed upon. They included rules like (1) while a member is speaking don't walk in front, hold sidebar conversations, or read a newspaper or pamphlet and (2) if two men rise to speak at the time, General Washington will determine the order in which they will speak. Knowing that there were a lot of talkers among the group (apparently an occupational hazard for politicians in every era!), a third rule said that on any given topic, a person could only speak two times. These rules helped ensure that the participants felt the kind of psychological safety they needed to confront difficult decisions.

Agile leaders consider the settings of their conversations from many vantage points. The physical location is important, but there are many other factors that will help participants build trust with one another and give their very best to the challenge at hand. When the topic of discussion is complex, the conversation will need to be deep and focused, and such conversations rarely happen without thoughtful planning.

A metaphor may be of use as you think about this. If you've ever done any serious hiking or river exploration you might have encountered a guide. A river guide or trail guide is going along the journey with those she is guiding. She assures everyone they will make camp by nightfall. She course-corrects as needed. She knows when to lead from behind, when to get out in front, and when to come alongside to encourage individuals. Above all, she keeps the members of the group safe. This is the role of the conversation guide as well, and why this skill of maintaining a safe environment for deep and focused conversation comes first. Use this skill on its own or combine it with some that come later in this book. Practice applying this skill in one-on-one conversations, in small groups and teams. In the next chapters, we give you some additional tools and insights to guide the conversation.

PUTTING THE SKILL TO WORK: THE AGILE LEADER AS CONVERSATION GUIDE

Agile leaders guide the conversation in ways that go beyond picking the right room or making sure that the group is the right size. The digital-age equivalent to "don't read a newspaper or pamphlet" during a deep, focused conversation might be "put your smartphones away." Common sense can dictate what the appropriate rules of civility should be when it comes to creating and maintaining a safe space for deep focused conversation. Our go-to rule of civility is this – *we will behave in ways that build trust and mutual respect*. It is not only the role of the agile leader to communicate and reinforce this rule, it is a shared responsibility among those having the conversation. This was also the case with at the Continental Congress. When a member was not acting in accordance with the established rules of civility, he could be "called to order" by any other member, as well as by George Washington.

This one rule of civility (or other rules that you may decide on for your own conversations) can certainly be *implied*, but in our work, we've seen that it is better to state the rule explicitly. Agile leadership means setting this expectation. One of the ways to do that is to help others understand that a strategic conversation is a specific kind of conversation that necessitates this sort of behavior – some of the regular ways in which people interact are suspended for the duration of the conversation for a particular purpose. Remember, deep focused conversations are not likely the sort of conversations most people are used to. Some may have developed conversational habits that are not conducive to doing the strategic, complex work that is hand. Your job is to help them develop new conversational habits.

Another simple conversational habit that can be implemented quite easily is *equity of voice*. When bringing together a small group or team for a strategic conversation explain that when individuals work together in groups, there is evidence that the best outcomes occur in groups that have the greatest levels of "equity of voice." This means that when they meet together, every member talks about the same amount of time. Simply letting group members know that you'll be striving for equity of voice can be quite powerful.

CASE STUDY: SETTING THE STAGE FOR DEEP CONVERSATIONS IN FLINT

Flint, Michigan, used to be a thriving city dominated by the auto industry. General Motors employed more than 80,000 people in Flint, and between GM and their suppliers the city enjoyed full employment and a thriving civic life. Any high school graduate knew that a good-paying job awaited them, allowing them to buy a home, raise a family, and send their children to college. When General Motors moved out of Flint in the 1980s, the city's population began a steep decline from a high of nearly 200,000 to approximately 97,000 today. As the economy declined, those who could get out – predominantly the middle and upper class – did, leaving the city with a high concentration of low-income and unemployed people. African Americans now constituted the majority and whites the predominant minority. The city was characterized by limited economic opportunity and desperate people just trying to survive. Housing challenges, limited healthy food options, racism, and poverty were (and continue to be) rampant.

We introduced you to the Flint team earlier. As you can imagine, the conversations that need to take place in that community are often painful and elicit strong emotions. The team's commitment to the skill of ensuring a safe space for deep and focused conversation has been instrumental in their work confronting the issues of poverty, violence, and entrenched institutional racism in Flint. One of the vehicles the team has been part of is a coalition called Neighbors Without Borders. Bob Brown (the Associate Director for the Center for Community and Economic Development at Michigan State University) introduced a Strategic Doing approach to the group, and the ways in which he's helped ensure a safe space have paved the way for deeper and deeper conversations about what it means to be a united community.

At one meeting that brought together Flint residents from every part of the city, Bob started out by suggesting that they get to know one another a bit. He asked them to take out business cards to aid that process – certainly not an uncommon tradition at many gatherings in countless communities. What came next, however, was far from traditional. Bob asked everyone to throw their cards into a trash can. The message: we each have something to contribute, even those of us who might not have a business card. In that room, everyone – from the foundation president to the man recently returned to the community from a long incarceration – would be equal contributors to the future they would build together.

NOTE

1. Psychological safety for those who were privileged enough to be invited to the conversation, that is. While the convention was unquestionably a success in that it held the country together in its infancy and laid out a framework in which it could flourish, with hindsight we also recognize the tremendous costs. Political scientist Robert Dahl highlighted the many shortcomings in his book, *How Democratic Is the American Constitution?* He cites a number of

major shortcomings, including the failure to provide voting rights to women, African Americans, and Native Americans; and the reliance on the electoral college in the election of the president. One of the convention's most complex challenges was dealing with the reality of slavery – an issue it handled by compromising in ways that kept slavery intact and protected until the Civil War more than 70 years later. We are still grappling with the consequences of those decisions – as author Jim Wallis suggests, racism is America's "original sin" and continues to beset each succeeding generation.

Chapter 3

FRAME THE CONVERSATION WITH THE RIGHT QUESTION (SKILL 2)

W hile on a family vacation in Santa Fe, New Mexico, a father and his three-year-old daughter were out for a stroll. While stopping to admire a particularly beautiful landscape, the father took a picture of his little girl against this lovely backdrop. This was long before the days of the smartphone camera. The girl had been told by her father many times that film had to be taken to a special store to be developed and that it would be several days before they could see their photographs. Although she knew this information, she asked the question anyway, as three-year-olds are so prone to do, "Why can't we see the picture right now?" Her father patiently offered the explanation yet again, but this time her question settled into his mind in a way it hadn't before . . . Why *can't* we see the picture right now?

Later, Edwin Land, founder of Polaroid, would recall that day in 1943 and he would add that "within an hour, the camera, the film, and the physical chemistry became clear." As an armchair physicist, he worked out in his head a new kind of photography system that would include all of the components of a conventional darkroom in a single handheld device – even before they returned from their walk. He called his patent attorney that same day. There was a certain power in the way in which his daughter asked her question. It caused Land to ask the question of himself, a question he had never really considered before. Questions can be powerful.

Every conversation begins with each person having an invisible frame around what they will discuss, a frame that sets the (usually subconscious) boundaries for them in the conversation. We need to bring these frames to the surface. Using the right question to do so can both open up new opportunities *and* keep the conversation focused in a productive direction.

David Cooperrider, professor of organizational behavior at Case Western Reserve University, says that "we live in the world our questions create." We spend time developing *framing questions* to assure we are all in the same world, as it were – looking as closely as we can at the same conversation. The second skill of agile leadership to design a conversation around an appreciative framing question, a question with many answers that will move the conversation in a positive direction. A good framing question is complex enough that it will require the deeper thinking and engagement of each person in

41

the conversation. That statement has many parts, so let's break it down into the elements of a good question, so that you will be able to ask the right questions in your conversations.

ADAPTIVE LEADERSHIP: ONE QUESTION, MANY ANSWERS

The work of Ronald Heifetz at Harvard University helps us think about the questions we might ask in a given situation. Heifetz labels questions as either *technical* or *adaptive*. When the problem definition, solution, and implementation is clear, Heifetz calls this a technical question. Confronted with a technical question, leaders can deploy expert knowledge and known thinking to lead them to the solution. Typically, there is one solution to a technical question. Answering a technical question often leads to an incremental improvement in current practices. Examples can include a city collecting all the trash each day on schedule, a company solving a quality problem to get the production line running again, or a government agency determining how to shorten waiting times at a public agency. Solutions to technical questions are not necessarily easy – all of these examples are ones that would require people (or a team) with considerable experience. But, with technical problems, leaders will engage a skilled person or team to find a solution *using their technical skills*.

Adaptive questions are different. They point us to challenges for which there are no clear answers. Adaptive questions can trigger many answers that might all lead to acceptable solutions. These types of questions have no known procedures or outcomes; they require a deeper questioning of fundamental assumptions and values. Solving adaptive questions requires us to exert significantly more effort, have a tolerance for uncertainty, and include the presence of divergent voices. Adaptive questions are also best addressed with the group that will be implementing the proposed solutions. We will need to engage others, and through their collective intelligence and strategic intuition. Learn our way toward possible solutions together. Here are some examples of adaptive questions: Is it possible for all students in the third grade to read at the third-grade level? How could we become the healthiest county in the state? Can we create a robust digital technology cluster?

How do we become the employer of choice in our industry? What is the best way to respond to a new technology that can erode our market position quickly? Each of these examples have many possible answers and each solution could contribute to that answer.

The adaptive leader develops the skill of asking clear, adaptive questions. These questions point a team, organization or community in a new direction. Being an adaptive leader requires you to be open to experimentation and innovation in order to generate answers to your adaptive questions. You will find that your experiments – your efforts to answer your adaptive question – are iterative. They cannot be fully planned before you begin. You will also find that as you let go of the urge to control, new solutions will appear. Exploring these potential solutions allows you to build new levels of trust and collaboration among the people who are part of the journey to discover new answers to adaptive questions.

We briefly discussed wicked problems in the first chapter. These are almost always adaptive challenges. You can think of wicked problems as those that you encounter that seem difficult or impossible – the characteristics of the problem keep you guessing as they change, and your knowledge may seem incomplete. They are not necessarily "evil" problems, but a wicked problem may seem to resist being solved, due to the many interconnections you find as you work to solve it. From their work in architecture and urban planning, the idea's originators (Rittel and Webber) wrote of wicked problems in public planning: public safety, education, transportation, affordable housing, health crises, conservation, and other social challenges. In recent years, the discussion has expanded as corporations facing globalization have realized they have their own wicked problems. To address these problems, they increasingly need to incorporate the diverse viewpoints of international customers and employees. We have found that the most productive way to address wicked problems begins by attracting diverse voices with a powerful *framing question*. These questions engage us. They set us off on a journey to find new opportunities to address these challenges.

If you're reading this book, you're probably faced with adaptive challenges. Your framing question, then, will need to acknowledge that reality. Good framing questions are adaptive questions. By their nature they seem big, bold, and inspiring. They grab the listener who wants to know more about how it will be accomplished and how they can be part of the solution. A good framing question is an invitation to deeper conversation that will lead to more questions, experimentation, and, ultimately, innovation.

What does such a question look like? Tina Seelig, of Stanford University's Department of Management Science and Engineering, and a faculty director of the Stanford Technology Ventures Program, demonstrates the power of reframing a question with a simple example. She starts with this question: What does 5 plus 5 equal? The answer, of course, is 10. We have an easy question with one answer. But what if we alter our question in this way: What two numbers equal 10? With this second question, we have an infinite number of possible answers. Seelig's point is a profound one: how we ask questions opens us to new possibilities. Our two questions differ only in the way they are framed.

In our organizations and communities, we are facing a growing number of adaptive challenges. As you confront these challenges you will want to ask a question that opens the door to infinite answers and new opportunities. You will also want to pose a framing question that connects to the unique combination of the people assembled to help you. Sound difficult? It takes practice. Adaptive leaders get really good at formulating compelling questions about a future we can't quite see yet.

APPRECIATIVE QUESTIONS

As we noted with the first skill, the core of Strategic Doing involves managing conversations. Why is that so? If we start with the idea that complex challenges require us to collaborate, then it is very difficult to see how we collaborate without having conversation. We need to be intentional in how we design and guide these conversations, because our actions will follow them. In other words, as Cooperrider also tells us, people move in the direction of their conversations – both for good and for ill. You can probably recognize this phenomenon from your own experience: you start out with an adaptive challenge – a wicked problem, perhaps – and you immediately begin diving into analyzing the cause of the problem. It can be a never-ending task, because, by definition, there is no single cause of a wicked problem. There is no single answer to an adaptive challenge. Take the example of climate change. Here's how a problem-centered conversation about climate change might evolve:

> Q. *Why is climate change occurring?*
> A. *Because people and companies pollute.*

> Q. *Why do people and companies pollute?*
> A. *Because they don't understand the consequences.*

> Q. *Why don't they understand the consequences?*
> A. *Because our schools don't teach them otherwise.*

> Q. *Why don't the schools teach them otherwise?*
> A. *Because they're too busy teaching basic reading and math.*

> Q. *Why are they too busy teaching reading and math?*
> A. *Because parents aren't doing their job.*

And so on – you get the idea. There is always a deeper level to the "because," as well as the opportunity to argue about whether the because is accurate or justified. Here's the important point: when we face an adaptive challenge – or a wicked problem – we should not engage in a problem-centric conversation. If we do, we are heading into an endless loop where nothing happens.

Cognitive psychology supports this idea that our conversations shape our actions. An individual's emotions and behavior follow the pattern of thought – the mental models – that we carry around in our heads. If our mental model interprets every situation as a problem to be solved, our conversation and behavior will be problem-focused. We will enter the endless loop of looking for problems to fix our complex adaptive challenges. However, cognitive psychology also tells us that we can shift these mental models. Our deeper conversations help us make these changes. If we focus on *opportunities*, we make sure that we do not fall into the ever-deepening chasm of problem analysis. We have the opportunity to think instead about possible alternatives.

Please don't misunderstand us – we are not discounting the value of exploring problems. It *is* important that we investigate the threat of climate change, or new disruptions to an existing business model, or why young people are leaving a region. However, we need to realize at the outset that we will *never* completely understand the causes of these kinds of wicked problems. We need to know *enough* – enough to engage in the conversation, and trust that we will learn more as we work together.[1] In meeting adaptive challenges, we learn by doing. So, we need conversations that lead us to action, to experimentation, so we can generate new insights into these complex situations.

Every conversation is in response to some question – whether that question is explicitly asked or not – and so choosing the right question makes an enormous difference. Problem-centered questions tend to bog groups down in analysis. We become paralyzed by the mistaken belief that there is one problem to solve. While a group might be able to sustain a litany of gripes for one meeting, no one wants to participate for long.

At the same time, we have a positive and equally important reason to ask opportunity-centered questions instead: they emotionally engage people. Truly complex problems will require that people are committed for the long haul. We need their engagement and insights. If we focus too much on an endless search for the "right" problem to solve, we exhaust people. We will end up pushing away the creative brain-power we need to address our adaptive challenges.

When we choose to seek out what is already good and right about an individual, team, or organization, then we have chosen an approach called *Appreciative Inquiry*, which was developed by Cooperrider. This approach is asset-based – positively focused – rather than deficit-focused – emphasizing problems. By developing framing questions that are appreciative, we set ourselves on the right path to find new opportunities and address our complex adaptive challenges.

DEVELOPING QUESTIONS TO FRAME CONVERSATIONS

Taking these concepts together – adaptive leadership and Appreciative Inquiry – you can use a question to frame a conversation so that the people you assemble are working together in new ways. A good framing question invites new levels of collaboration that lead to new solutions. It invites a new way of seeing and engaging others. Through a deeper conversation, you can move toward practical ways to address wicked problems. Think of it visually as building a picture frame within which you will create a new scene that no one person could create on their own. Appreciative framing questions open the door to new solutions to adaptive challenges. Steve Jobs was a master at asking powerful appreciative questions. He didn't ask, "How do we compete with IBM?" He asked, "What if computers were small and personal?" That powerful six-word question attracted the right team to build the computer that would make Apple a leader in innovation and design.

Developing a powerful framing question is not easy. For many of us, this change in thinking requires practice. Much of our schooling and experience trains us to look for problems, gaps, deficits, and deficiencies. We don't spend much time exploring what *could* be. We have difficulty imagining people mobilized to advance toward opportunities rather than spinning our wheels in problems. Even though your group or team may have been assembled because of a problem, practice approaching the conversation from a different perspective. Start from the position that everyone wants to build a more prosperous company, organization, or future. Invite them to start the journey to a new better solution.

You may find in your journey that people start by asking, "How can we do this?" or "How should we do that?" These questions may sound like they are opportunity-focused. Don't be deceived – as soon as you start using words like *can* and *should*, you're implying judgment and shutting off possibilities: Can we really do it? And should we? You can avoid this trap by substituting the word *might*: "How might we . . ." In this way, you're able to defer judgment, help people to create options more freely, and open more possibilities.

Let's look at two questions that illustrate what this skill looks like in practice. A company might be asked to consider this question: *What can we to do minimize customer anger and complaints?* This is an example of a nonappreciative question. It highlights what is clearly an issue for the organization asking it, but the group will work together more productively by considering a different question: *When have customers been most pleased with our service and what might we learn and apply from those moments of success?* The overall focus of the inquiry is on what the organization wants more of, not less.

A compelling framing question can inspire the group to an action that no one could see before the question was raised. An adaptive leader inspires new work by asking new questions. Questions that simply justify your current actions rarely lead to much improvement – especially when your current actions are not creating the results you want. The right framing question is enough to completely transform a conversation and to reboot a group that has gotten stuck. It leads us away from nonproductive mental models and sets the stage for transformation.

Use framing questions as an invitation to a conversation and a foundation for a productive collaboration. When you frame the right question, you can lead others (and yourself) to discover how shared value can be created together. By asking the right question – an appreciative one that allows for many perspectives on an adaptive challenge – agile leaders draw people into a deeper, more-focused conversation that can lead to many new opportunities. With the right framing question, participants will be eager to contribute their expertise and share other resources as they respond.

PUTTING THE SKILL TO WORK: THE AGILE LEADER AS QUESTIONER

One exercise to begin learning to ask good questions is to practice "How might" questions. Think of a question that describes a situation you want changed and ask yourself, "How might I improve this situation?" Begin your answers with "I could" or "What if I could do . . ." or "Imagine if . . ." If you try this approach in a group setting, you will be surprised how many answers can be generated in just a few minutes.

You can also practice your skills at asking better questions by selecting a topic and writing down as many questions as you can in a few minutes. Then look at your list. Sort them by technical versus adaptive questions. Now write a second list of questions. See if you have improved the questions with each round that you do.

A third exercise involves asking yourself – regularly – if your questions inspire others to contribute their time, ideas and energy. Chances are that if your questions are appreciative and focused on potential opportunities, you will engage people more easily than if you are continuously pointing out deficits.

If you are working with a group, the challenge of coming up with a good framing question is trickier. Getting to the framing question that a group wants to use is often an iterative process. Most of us are fully engaged in our daily work. Lifting our thinking to an adaptive question takes time. Don't be discouraged if the first question you come up with doesn't resonate. Ask a few colleagues to help, trying different perspectives and approaches until you find the right one. You might also use this checklist from Gervase R. Bushe of Simon Fraser University:

- Great questions are surprising. They are questions that people haven't discussed or thought about before.
- They are questions that cause people to reflect and think.
- They touch people's heart and spirit. They are questions that are personally meaningful and touch on that most matters to them.
- They prompt stories that will build relationships. As a result of the conversations these questions engender, people feel closer to each other. A greater sense of vulnerability and trust is achieved.
- They force us to look at reality a little differently. Sometimes reality can be reframed by the way a question is asked. (Bushe 2007)

You'll know when you have the right question – if questions invite people to conversation, the *right* question makes people say, "Yes! I'd love to be part of *that* conversation." Push through until you find the words that will bring people into the discussion with enthusiasm and purpose.

CASE STUDY: REFRAMING THE QUESTION AT A COMMUNITY INSTITUTION IN ROCKFORD

The Klehm Arboretum and Botanical Gardens in Rockford, Illinois was first established as a tree nursery in 1910. It was maintained as a nursery until 1985, when the Klehm family donated the nursery to Winnebago County and established it as an arboretum. Over time, the arboretum's board faced an ever-diminishing membership, higher maintenance costs, and lower event attendance. Community leaders that had been involved with the arboretum for many years had heard from some would-be members that the arboretum's location in a "less than desirable" neighborhood deterred many people from attending. The board decided that they needed a strategic plan to chart a more sustainable future.

Janyce was a former board member of the arboretum and was invited to help the board. She began by asking them to consider potential framing questions. Initial ideas focused on deficits such as a lack of members, low attendance, the rising cost of maintaining the grounds, and the inability to fund master plans. While all of these questions did touch on important aspects of the arboretum's operations, they were also focused on problems. Janyce pushed the conversation further, looking for an appreciative question. The turning point came when she asked them about their own experience – what inspired *them* about the arboretum? What were their first visits to the arboretum like? Why did they volunteer? This turned the discussion in a different direction: the board members began to reflect and share stories with one another, and remembered what it was that they loved about the arboretum. Eventually, the group settled on this framing question: "What would it look like if the beauty of our arboretum was shared?"

The board next invited their members to be part of this new conversation – one that was focused not on addressing a specific problem, but on imagining what was possible. Many members participated, generating lots of new ideas to help the arboretum move forward in four key areas: offering more family-friendly activities, boosting educational opportunities, improving reputation, and building lifelong memories for visitors. The conversations re-energized members' commitments to the arboretum and its future, and the first facility enhancements are now underway: a new garden pavilion and terrace are complete, new signage has been installed, and a children's garden is currently under construction.

NOTE

1. It is for this reason that we usually discourage the Strengths/ Weaknesses/Opportunities/Threats (SWOT) exercise that is the customary kickoff to traditional strategic planning. In our experience, a group almost always already knows enough about the weaknesses and threats to move forward. We discuss this further in the next chapter.

Chapter 4

IDENTIFY YOUR ASSETS, INCLUDING THE HIDDEN ONES (SKILL 3)

M any people operate in what we might call "If Only Land." Every time they are part of a conversation, they are quick to bring up what they wish they had – a better job, a nicer home, more well-behaved children. Companies and organizations aren't much different. If you could listen in on their meetings, you'd hear statements like:

If only we hadn't missed that opportunity . . .
If only we had more money . . .
If only other countries didn't have such low labor costs . . .

it's not that these desires aren't real – the people and organization truly would like to be in a different position. But at the end of the conversation, nothing's changed, and most likely, the next time you talk, you'll hear the same sentiments over again.[1]

If we're honest with ourselves, it's not just other people in "If Only Land." Most of us are at least frequent visitors. We've convinced ourselves that we can't really do anything until someone else acts to fill a need that we see as critical. It's not necessarily that we are pessimistic by nature (although that may be the case for some of us). It's really a manifestation of hierarchy thinking. We've discussed the ways in which hierarchies limit thinking and control behavior; another of their important functions is to allocate resources. Most organizations have a number of processes around this: budgeting, for example, allows leaders to provide funding to various units. "Stage-gating," in which groups present new project ideas in a prescribed fashion for approval to go forward, is another. More generally, we are accustomed to looking to someone who has more authority than we do to provide the things we need.

Skill 3 asks us to give up that perspective. In network thinking, there is no top or bottom. We may still need resources, but there is no one whose job it is to give them to us. We need first to take stock of the resources we *already* have. What do we, and the members of our network that have agreed to work with us, have to offer to address the question we're asking? This isn't just (perhaps overly) optimistic thinking; as you'll see, in a network environment, it is exceptionally practical. We have resources all around us that can be used in new and different ways.

ASSETS

We use the word *assets* to describe these resources. An asset is any resource that could potentially be put to work to help us move toward a particular outcome. When we hear the word asset, those of us who have taken an accounting course immediately think in terms of money – the side of the balance sheet that offsets liabilities. However, assets come in many different varieties, and go far beyond cash. If you limit your perspective to funding, you will have a hard time getting out of "If Only Land."

In identifying assets, it can be helpful to think in terms of different categories. Depending on the challenge you're trying to address, specific categories may be more or less valuable. Here's one way to organize assets, with some examples in each area:

Physical and natural assets: These assets include things like real estate (land or buildings), meeting spaces, water rights, classrooms, large or specialized equipment, or high-speed fiber. There are also cyber-equivalents for some of these: virtual meeting rooms, for example.

Skill and knowledge assets: Again, the specifics depend on the context, but these could include skills in writing, graphic design, public speaking, budgeting, website construction, research, or cooking, among many others. Although related but slightly different, knowledge assets could include subject matter expertise as well as assets from which new knowledge and insights can be gained. These could include data sets and algorithms.

Social assets: Social assets are individual people or groups of people with whom someone in your network is personally acquainted. Professional organizations, an entrepreneur with a technology that complements your company's, the mayor, or a well-known author are all examples of social assets.

Capital assets: While we don't want to limit our thinking to money, we certainly can't forget about it either. Capital assets are financial resources or assets that otherwise would be bought, such as editorial space in a newspaper for an opinion column, or administrative support that someone could donate to the cause.

As you think about what assets you or your group have, you might not be sure what category they belong in. That's okay – the categories are primarily meant to help you expand your thinking about the assets you have at your disposal. With these categories, we are simply asking you to think broadly and more horizontally.

There is a common thread to both Skill 2 (asking the right question) and this one (identifying our assets): both rest on the principle that we move in the direction of our conversations. In "If Only Land"we focus on our problems and what we do not have – it is a one-way trip to the cul-de-sac of inaction. It may momentarily feel good to vent to one another, but ultimately it saps our energy and potential for change. Focusing on what we do have – our assets – helps us change our focus to the opportunities that lie before us. It is an appreciative approach. In community development, this perspective has changed the way work is done in struggling neighborhoods and communities. Instead of defining the challenge as a lack (not enough money, not enough two-parent families, bad infrastructure, etc.), "asset-based community development" challenges civic leaders to ask a different question. What could we do with the assets to which we already have access? What does our neighborhood already have? Perhaps we have a network of churches willing to work together on new afterschool programs, or a group of young people interested in starting their own businesses. Those assets become the starting point for the work of transformation. The skill of identifying assets keeps us focused on talking about opportunities, not problems.

This same mind-set is also important for companies. For a new business venture, financial resources and a large staff aren't available, so entrepreneurs need to seek other approaches. Who do we know with the skills or connections that might help us move forward? In larger companies, corporate assets tend to be locked away within departmental and business unit budgets. There is often little thought of sharing these assets across organizational boundaries. Because of this dynamic, strategy has become moribund in many companies. We see strategy discussions that have degenerated into more routine budgeting exercises, all designed to protect what managers already have and to get a little more.

In the nonprofit world and government, the ignorance of our assets shows up in a different way. We've been in more than one situation where multiple nonprofits are working in the same geographic region, a city or even a neighborhood, and they don't know each other. As a result, they have no idea of the range of assets that exist across nonprofit organizations to deal with shared social problems. In one midsized Midwestern city, for example, we convened all the nonprofits that received funding from the city government. Oddly, it was the first time that they had sat in the same room together.

GUIDELINES FOR IDENTIFYING ASSETS

As you try to identify the assets that might be useful for whatever challenge it is you're addressing, you need to keep a few things in mind. First, *direct influence* is critical. If it's not your asset, it's (to be blunt) *not* an asset. While it may be wonderful that your Uncle Mortimer's ex-wife's cousin is an expert in social media, that skill is probably not readily available to your group. Assets have to be either resources you personally own, or that you at least exert significant control over. For example, while you may not own a 3-D printer yourself, if you're easily able to reserve time on one where you work, then that is an asset that you can legitimately contribute.

Second, each person makes *autonomous decisions* about sharing assets. Sometimes a member just doesn't want to make an asset available for whatever reason. A prominent member of the community, for example, may be tired of being asked to be introduced to a city official. A professional photographer has decided "no more" to any requests for *pro bono* services. Those decisions may be temporary ones or more permanent, but either way, they are decisions that need to be respected.

Finally, true assets are *actionable* – that is, we can describe them in a way that makes it clear how we might use them. In working on developing a new technology, someone may tell us, "I know lots of people who have experience with testing new products." Is this a useful "social" asset? We can't tell – asking more questions will help us figure it out: What kinds of products? In which markets? Who are the specific people that the person knows well that might be approached?

Beyond these guidelines, keep an open mind about whether something is really an asset – you don't need to know exactly how it could be used to address a challenge. As long as there's a plausible case to be made that it might be relevant, keep it in mind as a potential resource to take advantage of.

HIDDEN ASSETS

Some people think they have no assets. Perhaps they aren't in a position of authority in the organization, or they're a high school student or retired person. If you simply ask them "What are your assets?" they may reply "Nothing," or, "I'm not even sure why I'm here." We can confidently say from years of experience that *everyone* has assets, and often the most valuable assets are the ones that no one thought of at first. Many assets are hidden – sometimes there is no one else in the group with any idea that the person has that asset. Some of our assets are hidden even from ourselves – it takes another person to draw them out and identify the value they can have to the group.

Common hidden assets are hobbies, skills, or interests someone has pursued independently over the years. One of our favorite examples is from a project Ed worked on. A group was thinking about ways to address a common problem: how to develop a workforce with the skills for twenty-first-century manufacturing. They discussed what assets they had to develop some kind of initiative. One member of the group somewhat reluctantly shared that she was interested in both manufacturing and sustainability. A little gentle prodding revealed that she also had experience in curriculum design. That conversation led to the first national "green collar" certification of manufacturing workers. The group was so engaged by her hidden assets that they rallied around to get this new program started.

ASSETS ARE STARTING POINTS

If you've ever been part of an improvisation class or workshop, you may be familiar with the phrase, "Bring a brick, not a cathedral." In improv, the phrase means that each person adds only a few actions or lines to move the plot forward – they don't have to finish the whole "story." For our purposes, the phrase reminds us that no one has to have a fully formed concept for a new opportunity, initiative, or project – in fact, it's usually better when we *don't* have a complete idea in mind. We start from an open-minded posture, in which each person can say, "This is what I have – a few bricks." What can be built from them will emerge as we work together.

You may feel as the assets you and your colleagues can contribute to an adaptive challenge are just not sufficient – it seems like quite a meager set of resources in the face of a big issue. This is in some ways true – you *don't* have everything you need (remember, that's the very nature of an adaptive challenge, as opposed to a technical one). However, the flip side of this disadvantage is a powerful truth: because you are only working with what you have, you can start work *right now*. You don't need permission. You don't have to wait for more funding or people or legislation. You are free to move ahead. As you'll see, something almost magical happens when you seize the opportunities available to you. Agile leaders understand this paradox of scarcity and opportunity, and they move forward with confidence.

PUTTING THE SKILL TO WORK: THE AGILE LEADER AS INVENTORY TAKER

Using this skill can be as simple as taking out a sheet of paper or a set of sticky notes and asking yourself and the other people with whom you are working to list assets. Use the four categories to spur your thinking – in which categories are you "asset-rich"? Where might you be missing some assets? Ask questions that might unearth those hidden assets that you did not even know were there.

Each of the people in your group will bring their own set of assets. Sometimes they are assets that are really truly their own (for example, someone is a graphic designer), and sometimes they are assets that they can exert control over (there's video equipment at their school that they could check out to use). If you know each other well, you can prod a bit to remind one another of assets they might have left out – as in the example of the team member interested in sustainability. However, remember that members of your group have autonomy – they can decide whether to make the asset available to others. Maybe they are tired of always being asked to design the website – or they don't yet trust the group enough to invest their time in this way. As you think about what assets your network has, keep your focus on what you can reasonably expect to control that has been made available.

This isn't to say that you should list any and every asset. Sometimes an asset truly has no value to a network: a collection of stuffed animals for a group designing a new business process, say. If it seems like people's contributions aren't quite hitting the mark, revisit your framing question, if you have one (if you don't, you might consider taking a time-out to develop one). Assets should have some possible connection to the challenge you're working on – to your framing question – even if you can't quite see what the connection would be. When in doubt, err on the side of inclusion.

Even so, after you've finished making your inventory, you may feel like your list is pretty short. Don't panic – part of the genius of networks is that the set of available assets is not static. Every new person that comes into the network brings new assets with them. Every boundary spanner in your network can help you identify other networks that can make needed assets available. Every cautious pragmatist that comes on board may decide that they do, in fact, trust the group enough to cash in on that favor someone owes them. Keep asking yourself (and others) what new assets you have that you might be willing to share. The assets you have to work with will grow as you work.

Agile leaders help surface potential that the group didn't know existed by focusing on assets. They focus a network on what can be done, rather than wallowing in its problems or waiting for someone else to act. Even when the resources seem inadequate, knowing what they are means that the group can start building with those bricks, thinking creatively about using them to create new opportunities.

CASE STUDY: REIMAGINING AN IT DEPARTMENT

In 2015 a global life sciences company contacted the Purdue team with a challenge – rethinking the role of their information technology (IT) department. Historically, they (like most companies) had viewed IT largely as a cost center. Information technology, human resources, accounting, and other "service" units are often viewed as part of overhead, or even a drain on profits – although the function is obviously essential to a company's performance. The company's leadership wondered if it was possible to use the department's assets not just to "service" the IT needs of others throughout the company, but also to create additional revenue. They hired a large outside firm to develop a next-generation strategy for IT. The recommendation of the outside firm was very complex and the company's leadership was unsure how to implement it.

Scott knew an internal strategy consultant at the company, and through that relationship met the leadership of the IT department. Scott proposed assisting the IT department in considering how it might go beyond being a cost center by considering how its assets could be tapped to generate revenue for the company.

The first step was for the department to identify what assets they had that could contribute to new opportunities. Many of the assets shared were ones that you would expect to find in an IT department: various types of hardware, knowledge of business software applications, programming expertise, and so on. Scott suggested that workshop participants include in their thinking assets they had, which others might not be aware of. As is the case with many groups, the participants had been thinking exclusively within their work contexts, so Scott helped prime the pump by asking whether anyone had special knowledge or skills because of a hobby or other personal passion. At this prompt, one participant, Joe, mentioned tinkering with animation software as an asset he could contribute.

Animation was not part of Joe's job, but he had been interested in the growth of this relatively new field (relatively new, that is, in its application to business). He'd begun reading up on it, and had purchased a software package and begun developing his own skills. This animation capability ended up being integral to a project that the group moved forward to develop – a new value-added, revenue-generating service they could offer to their customers.

It's worth noting that in this case, identifying a heretofore unidentified asset paid off for the company, but it also opened up new opportunities for Joe. As the person on the team with the most expertise in this area, he now had the opportunity to use his new skills in a reconfigured position that focused explicitly on animation.

NOTE

1. The region that shares a border with "If Only Land"is "The Republic of SWOT." Mentioned briefly in the last chapter, we're often asked where SWOT (Strengths, Weaknesses, Opportunities, Threats) analyses fit into our work. The risk of visiting the Republic of SWOT is that you overstay your visit . . . in other words, you can spend weeks and months on a SWOT analysis. In fact, a common delaying tactic of the skeptic or sorehead is to suggest that what a group really needs to do is a SWOT analysis. Indeed, we've heard people say that we cannot take any action *without* a SWOT analysis. There is a time and a place for a SWOT analysis – but in most cases, we've found that groups have already identified the Weaknesses and Threats that face them. More attention is not useful, at least at the outset; they know enough to begin working to do something. This skill and the one in the next chapter focus on the more valuable parts of a SWOT analysis – the Strengths and Opportunities – although we narrow the focus on both of these dimensions as well, so that the effort spent on them is as valuable as possible.

Chapter 5

LINK AND LEVERAGE ASSETS TO IDENTIFY NEW OPPORTUNITIES (SKILL 4)

In the previous chapter, we discussed the power of uncovering hidden assets, both in yourself and in others, and we alluded to an old adage of improvisational theater, "bring a brick, not a cathedral." In this chapter, we offer another lesson from improv. "Yes, and" is considered the first rule of improvisation. In an improvisational skit, it means that when a fellow performer offers something – a line, for instance – the other performers accept the line as stated. That's the "yes" part. Then another actor expands on it. That's the "and." For example, suppose one person started an improvised scene by saying, "Can you believe Maria is just dropping everything and headed to Australia for three months?" The next person would accept that as fact in the scene and build on it; they might continue the story with, "Yes, and apparently she's had a lifelong interest in learning to play the digeridoo." The story would continue with each performer accepting what has come before and building on it. There is no way to tell where the story of Maria will end up.

Agile leaders not only uncover hidden assets, they also see how different assets could be linked, leveraged, and aligned, and can help others see that potential as well. A mere list of assets is not enough. The magic happens when assets get combined.[1] Combining assets can create new value that is greater than the combined value of the parts. Doing so is a skill; in this chapter we provide some guidance to help you do just that. Making these kinds of connections is useful in many contexts, but is critical in a network (rather than a hierarchy) – it provides the platform from which collective solutions to our most complex challenges will emerge.

LINKING AND LEVERAGING ASSETS TO INNOVATE

Linking and leveraging assets can help us be more innovative. Here's an example of linking and leveraging assets in action:

It was Saturday of the Fourth of July weekend and the restaurant was packed. Every table was full and had been all day long. The line of hungry customers never seemed to get any shorter. Provisions were beginning to run low, including some of the key ingredients for the two salads offered on the menu. Not wanting to miss any sales or disappoint customers, the owner thought fast, pulling a few items from the shelves, putting them on a cart, and wheeling the cart into the bustling dining room. He took the cart to each table where a salad had been ordered and said that even though they were out of the two menu salads, they were in for a very special treat: a new house salad, prepared and served tableside. With the flair of a magician the owner placed leaves of romaine lettuce into a bowl, adding a drizzle of olive oil, Worcestershire sauce, a squeeze of a lemon, and two coddled eggs. He added salt, pepper, and grated Parmesan cheese with a few flicks of his wrist. Rather than tossing the ingredients he gently folded them, coating each leaf with the creamy dressing. The salads were plated, croutons added, and served to the hungry diners.

The owner called the salad *The Aviator* in honor of the many Navy airmen who made their way over the border from San Diego to eat at the establishment: Caesar Cardini's Tijuana restaurant. It would be a few years before it became known as the Caesar Salad, invented on July 4, 1924.

We love this story for a couple of reasons. First, who doesn't love a great origin story, even if it's a recipe origin story? Although it is in a different location now, Caesar's is still in operation and still preparing their famous salad and serving it tableside. The other reason we love this story is because it is a story of innovation, specifically *recombinant innovation*. Let's stick with food to help further illustrate this notion.

In a 2015 journal article, Italian researchers recounted their work looking to chefs to learn some lessons about innovation. They were specifically interested in how new dishes were developed. The research found that among Italy's top chefs, new dishes usually feature a combination of separate ingredients that the chefs have used for a long time, but have put *together* for the first time in the new dish.

For instance, a chef might have been using pumpkin in several desserts over the years. He also had a great gorgonzola blue cheese that he used in a salad, and, of course, every Italian chef uses a lot of fresh herbs. Then, one day when the chef was thinking about a new dish for the fall, he came up with a recipe for Pumpkin Gnocchi with Gorgonzola and Crispy Sage. The gnocchi was a big hit – so popular that the restaurant was able to charge a premium price that yielded a higher than normal profit margin. This pattern appeared over and over: taking ingredients the chefs were very familiar with and combining them in a previously untested way. There was an additional finding: often, one more ingredient was present in those popular new dishes, an ingredient that was completely new to the chef's repertoire, often an obscure flavor they had encountered when traveling to a different part of the world or that was brought to the chef's attention by a kitchen's staff member from another culture. That's what is meant by recombinant innovation: taking things that already exist and combining them in new ways.

This is also what we mean when we talk about *linking and leveraging* assets. Let's go back to Caesar Cardini's restaurant for a moment. When faced with hungry diners, Caesar did a quick inventory: he had romaine lettuce, eggs, olive oil, lemons, croutons. He had a cart he could wheel into the dining room. He also had a couple of skills: knowledge about the basic components of a salad dressing (an oil and an acid), and critically, a flair for the dramatic. Put all these together, and you have a dish that has continued to command a premium price as a "special" dish for almost a century.

Since most of us are not chefs, here's an example from the world of technology: GPS or global positioning systems, are a remarkable innovation that link, leverage, and align satellite technology with atomic clock technology with radio transmitter and receiver technology. Those technologies were separate assets, probably each resident as bodies of knowledge in different experts' heads. The assets didn't align themselves automatically. When someone (probably a group of someones) wondered, "What if we combined them?," a breakthrough in modern navigation was imminent.

Sometimes these breakthroughs happen serendipitously, or seemingly so, but you can follow a discipline to help structure that serendipitously. The right framing question, for instance, can serve as the invitation for conversation to those people who might hold one of those key assets in their heads. A safe space is also important in order to have the deep focused conversation to explore the possibilities. Agile leaders can then help people see the opportunities that emerge when we begin to link, leverage, and align our collection of assets.

How important is this skill? Think about this: the emerging *Internet of Things* allows us to connect anything with anything through a digital link. On the factory floor, RFID tags guide a production line to customize each item according to the preferences of individual consumers who have placed online orders. Our automobile can signal to a billboard to advertise the next gas station when we're running low. In the kitchen, our refrigerator can order milk when we are almost out and have it delivered. Our opportunities to link, leverage, and align assets are literally endless. Individuals who understand and can put in practice processes such as recombinant innovation will lead the world to places we can't even begin to imagine today.

LINKING AND LEVERAGING ASSETS FORCE US TO THINK HORIZONTALLY

Many of us have a natural tendency to think vertically – that is, to explore specific topics in depth. Experts in any discipline are by definition good vertical thinkers. Academics and technologists can be especially prone to vertical thinking. Vertical thinking is useful when we need to reflect deeply about things. It is also, however, helpful to think horizontally, across different disciplines, fields, or bodies of knowledge. New insights can occur when we think horizontally. At Purdue, for example, there is a group called the Regenstrief Center for Healthcare Engineering (RCHE). Here horizontal thinking occurs on a daily basis; in fact, it was horizontal thinking that resulted in the idea for RCHE, in response to the appreciative question, *How might we improve the healthcare system by bringing engineers together with nurses and pharmacists?* "Healthcare Engineering" as a field of practice and research was born. Engineers have assets. Nurses have assets. Pharmacists have assets. Linking and leveraging those assets requires horizontal thinking.

Here's how all this works in practice: let's take the example of infusion pumps. These are the devices that hang by the bedside in a hospital and deliver fluids, such as nutrients and medications, into a patient's body. While these pumps provide a high degree of accuracy in the delivery of medications, there are also significant safety problems. Malfunctions can result in the overdelivery or underdelivery of medication. RCHE has established the infusion pump informatics community of practice among more than 100 hospitals in the Midwest. Through a web-based tool, these hospitals can now share data, analysis, and best practices to improve patient safety.

Sometimes horizontal thinking occurs as in the RCHE story, when people who look at the world differently get together. In other instances, an individual (whether by design or serendipitously) learns something about another field or context, and they are led to a new insight. A number of authors have written excellent books exploring the power of horizontal thinking. Franz Johansson calls the creation of insights at the intersection of different fields and cultures "the Medici effect." Stephen Johnson, in his wonderful book *Where Good Ideas Come From*, shatters the myth that innovation comes from a "Eureka!" moment. Instead, good ideas emerge over time out of different patterns of connection. Johnson identifies seven of these patterns. One he calls the "adjacent possible." In describing how incubators have evolved, Johnson points out that innovations can come from exploring the edges of what currently exists. Each advancement of the incubator over its 140-year history relied on recombining existing parts originally designed for other purposes. Through this recombination, a new idea emerges. We cannot leave this section, though, without pointing to the remarkable work of science historian James Burke. In his book *Connections* (and a companion television series), Burke traces multiple innovations through history to show how ideas jump from one field to another. An agile leader develops the skills to do each of these things: to see assets in different domains and spot their intersections and or connection possibilities, as well as to bring people together to reveal their hidden assets and then spot the link-and-leverage opportunities.

DEVELOPING YOUR ABILITY TO THINK HORIZONTALLY

If you are not someone for whom thinking horizontally comes naturally, there is good news. This is a skill that can be learned. Imagine you are working on a real "head-scratcher," trying to solve a particularly perplexing problem. This is a good time to take a *thought walk*.

The idea of a thought walk comes from engineer and creativity expert Michael Michalko.

A thought walk could be a quick loop around the office; on a nice day it might take you outside to the parking lot, or maybe even to run a few errands. A thought walk could even be a thought "drive" or subway trip. Wherever it is that you go, note things you come across randomly, pick up, or purchase. In the office it might be the water fountain or a tape dispenser. On a walk outside, you possibly encounter sounds of birds chirping, the daffodils that are starting to bloom, a discarded water bottle, or just about anything else. On an errand it could be the items you pick up at the store.

Don't look for things that are related to the problem or idea you are working on, rather, select items with no apparent connection to your problem or idea and no apparent relationship to one another. When you return from your thought walk jot down the characteristics of the items you encountered or acquired. For that tape dispenser, you might write down words like *sticky, transparent, spinning*. Now try to find a connection between one or more of the characteristics and the problem or idea you are working on. Here's an example from author Michalko of how a thought walk generated new insights for one engineer.

An engineer was working on safe and efficient ways to remove ice from power lines during ice storms. He had run out of ideas and none of the ones he had seemed right. He took a break and went for a walk. On his walk, he visited a store that had several different varieties of honey for sale in a variety of different containers. The store advertised the honey with a cutout of a large bear holding a jar of honey. He bought a jar to take home and returned to his office.

At his desk, while simultaneously thinking of honey, the cutout bear, and his power line problem, he came up with a pretty "out there" solution. Imagine, he thought, putting a honey pot on top of each power pole. This would attract bears and the bears would climb the poles to get to the honey. Their climbing would cause the poles to sway and the ice would vibrate off the wires. Although this was a silly idea, it led him to think about the phenomenon of vibration, which led him to a vibration-related solution. The solution the power company implemented was to bring in helicopters to hover over the iced power lines. Their hovering vibrated the ice off the power lines. The solution had nothing at all to do with either honey or bears, but he may not have gotten there without them (Michalko, n.d.).

GUIDING A GROUP TO THINK HORIZONTALLY

When a group of people begins to think horizontally they are literally thinking together – and thinking together is a fascinating phenomenon. When we think horizontally together we are actually creating an *extended mind*. This idea was first introduced by philosopher Andy Clark and cognitive scientist David Chalmers. According to Clark and Chalmers, a person's mind and cognitive processing are not limited to their head or even their body. The extended mind extends into the person's world, including to objects. For example, the use of to-do lists to augment one's memory is a simple way of way of extending the mind. Of course, we also use other, much more sophisticated storage and retrieval devices like computers and the internet to extend our minds.

In their book *The Knowledge Illusion: Why We Never Think Alone*, Steven Sloman and Philip Fernbach build on the extended mind theory, noting that one's mind also extends to the people around them. Furthermore, we are constantly drawing on information and expertise stored outside our heads: in our environment, our possessions, and the community with which we interact. What we might call "assets" are thus everywhere.

As we saw in Chapter 4, our approach to designing and guiding complex collaborations begins by identifying assets that could contribute to potential solutions – skill assets, physical assets, capital assets, social assets. When we do this with a group, we are essentially mapping our collective extended mind. We invariably end up with a rich collection of assets. The team can then draw on these varied assets to design an array of possible solutions.

Say a group of five to seven individuals has been tasked with designing a strategy to address a complex issue. If each person identifies five assets the group then has 25 to 30 assets in their collective asset inventory. As we saw in Chapter 1 when we looked at the innovation of the telephone, mixing and matching different combinations of these assets to form potential solutions gives us a nearly endless set of possibilities.

Complex challenges will require us to consider and experiment with many different strategies or options. We can build that list by taking our assets and combining them in different ways. This approach is a simple but effective way to achieve the variety of options needed to deal with complex challenges. If we identify our assets, even those that are hidden, we can connect them. Connecting them allows us to literally think horizontally together. Linking and leveraging assets by thinking horizontally and helping others to do it as well is a skill that can be learned. Solutions to today's complex challenges will not be developed in hierarchies. They will be designed in networks that link and leverage assets. They will be designed collectively by thinking horizontally, and they will be designed with the help of agile leaders.

PUTTING THE SKILL TO WORK: THE AGILE LEADER AS CONNECTOR

The skill of linking and leveraging assets is one that some people find easier than others – the natural horizontal thinkers take to it quickly – but it's also a skill that can be strengthened through practice. To begin, you could start with identifying a small set of assets – perhaps a few assets in each of the categories from the last chapter. Select three to four at random and see if you can come up with a way in which they could be combined – a hypothetical new product, service, program, or initiative that might have some value. Suspend your evaluative instincts and go for quantity over quality. When you've exhausted the possibilities for your first set of three to four assets, repeat with another set. You can use this same technique "in real life." Devote some time to simply brainstorming new possibilities from combining the assets you have at your disposal – if you're stuck, pick out a few at random and ask, "What if we combined these?" "What about these?" With even a few assets, the number of possibilities you can create will surprise you.

CASE STUDY: LINKING AND LEVERAGING ASSETS TO BUILD A CUTTING-EDGE INDUSTRY CLUSTER

Milwaukee, situated on Lake Michigan and at the confluence of three rivers, is Wisconsin's largest city and the fifth largest in the Midwestern United States. The city was dominated by manufacturing until 1970. Many of the industries traditionally associated with Milwaukee, such as beer breweries, leveraged the ready availability of water to fuel their growth. Following the significant decline of manufacturing in the region, city leaders began to consider how to grow a new economy. In 2007, government leaders reached out to the University of Wisconsin, Milwaukee, to consider possibilities for drawing on water assets to create a twenty-first-century economy.

In July 2008, the university contacted Ed and invited him to conduct a workshop with the Milwaukee Water Council to identify opportunities for the city to become a global leader in freshwater technologies. Participants knew even before the workshop that Milwaukee was home to laboratories and businesses that individually addressed different aspects of the full water cycle – from water delivery (faucets and toilets), to water measurement and metering, to water reuse and purification, to wastewater and sewage filtration. But what to do with that information? Participants began to imagine possibilities for linking and leveraging their own assets into collaborations that could fuel the development of new freshwater technologies and establish Milwaukee as a global hub for water-related industry. One such possibility became a reality even before the workshop was over: two CEOs offered to make their research labs available to any start-up company in freshwater technology. Immediately, Milwaukee had a powerful new asset to accelerate the formation of new companies. This seemingly small step showed everyone that much more could be done by linking and leveraging assets, and more commitments quickly followed.

Today, the Water Council has become a global leader in freshwater technology. The initial set of assets identified helped jump-start the council's work, and in the last decade many new assets have been established through the collaborative efforts that started at that first workshop. The city is now home to more than 200 water technology businesses, many in a new "Water Technology District" in a formerly dormant neighborhood. Milwaukee now boasts water research labs for public–private collaborations, a water technology park to nurture water-related businesses, and the nation's first school of freshwater sciences. Since 2010, total investment in the Water Technology District is more than $210 million, with private investments totaling just over half of that amount. Property values in the district have increased by more than 16%, bucking the trend of a decrease in property values in the city as a whole given the national recession. Given the growing importance of water management in an era of global climate change, the economic future of Milwaukee is very bright indeed.

NOTE

1. This is another shortcoming of the SWOT analysis. The "strengths" quadrant can be thought of as an inventory of our assets. While it's useful to know what we have, the inventory really only tells us the fixed value of each individual asset at a particular moment in time.

Chapter 6

LOOK FOR THE "BIG EASY" (SKILL 5)

O ur days are full of choices. Decisions – what, where, or when to eat, among others – face us every day. What to wear, where to go, what purchase is next, what color to paint the room, what flower to plant are just some of our many choices that seem simple to make. Some choices are more complex: What school should my child attend, should I take a job in another state, how do I invest for the best return, should I run for political office? All of these are questions we could encounter.

Individual choices are up to each of us. We decide what is best for ourselves. We may ask for input, but we in the end the choice is ours. But especially when we are part of a group and must make a choice, we look for ways that will be are fair to all involved and will meet the goals that the group has set for itself.

In Chapter 5, you learned about combining assets into opportunities. Assets can be combined to create a limitless set of opportunities, for all practical purposes. This is good news, but we can't do everything at once. To develop and implement an effective strategy, we must move at least one of our ideas to action. The reason is simple: our resources are limited. Often teams can get stuck at this point by ruminating about choices and what should come first. The fifth skill an agile leader needs involves efficiently sorting through many options to identify one that has the best chance of success.

DECISION-MAKING METHODOLOGIES

You've probably used many different methods to deal with this challenge; here's a rundown of some of the most common. The first is *consensus*, in which everyone agrees to support a particular decision. The assumption is that this is in the best interest of the whole. The selected option may not be the favorite of each person but is the one the group as a whole will support. A dictionary might define consensus (at its best) as a sense of unity around a belief or proposed action. Consensus can be hard to achieve; groups that insist on it for philosophical reasons may find themselves taking a very long time trying to reach it. A modification of the consensus method takes into account that you may have one vocal individual who insists on their choice, while everyone else has coalesced around a different choice. This alternative is called *consensus minus one*. Everyone must agree, except one person. If that one person cannot convince another, we move ahead. But if at least two people do not agree with the majority, the group cannot yet move forward. The assumption behind this method is that if two people oppose a choice, there's probably some good reason. More conversation needs to take place.

Alternatively, you could vote, and let the *majority's choice* carry the day. This has the advantage of being straightforward. However, if the vote is close, you run the risk of continually being dragged back into a discussion about whether the choice was *really* the right one. A variation of the majority vote method (particularly if you are choosing among a large number of options) is to give each person a number of votes; each person can allocate as many of their votes as they want to any particular choice. One common way to do this is *"sticky dot" voting*, in which you give each person a number of small colored adhesive dots to use to cast their votes on a large piece of paper listing the options, and they can divide their dots among choices as they'd like. The items with the most votes (dots) rise to the top for more discussion and then a decision.

Majority choice voting has a significant shortcoming: each person is (generally) using one criterion to make their choice. They're thinking to themselves things like:

That one would be quick.
This wouldn't cost very much; let's choose it.
That idea would be the most popular with our customers.

This shortcoming hides two deeper problems: first, there's been no discussion about what the criterion is or should be. The second is that if the challenge is really an adaptive one, thinking about things in light of only one factor is probably too simplistic. Some groups recognize this problem, and set up a very elaborate rating system in which every idea is evaluated using several criteria. Then all the ratings are totaled, sometimes weighted so that one or more criteria count more than others, and a "winner" is announced. This seems scientific enough, but in our experience, it's more trouble than it's worth. It can take the rest of the meeting, or even longer, just to set up the rating system (there are exceptions: in our work with NASA's life scientists, a complex rating system was unavoidable. There were a number of different factors, such as crew time on the International Space Station, budget burn rates, and the extent of the existing scientific knowledge base that participants had to consider).

All of these approaches to decision-making have merit in particular circumstances. In choosing one of these, you are ensuring that decisions are made in a fair and transparent way – that is, there are no "backroom deals." When the group considers the process fair, trust grows. As it does, the group's performance will improve.

Think back on a time when your enthusiasm for a project lagged and you may discover that the root cause was a lack of trust in the fairness of the process. People may not initially support a chosen idea, but if the process is fair their support can be earned. This fairness rule in selecting between options is key to the speed and success of implementation. When working with a group of people, especially when they do not report to each other but want to accomplish a difficult task together, building an open and fair process takes time and careful consideration of each person's views. In the long run this preparation work assures enthusiasm and desire for success by the team members implementing the agreed-upon task.

In hierarchical organizations where the decisions are made above and then implemented below, there is less personal commitment to execution. The "back room" made the decision so your ownership is low (and the level of office gossip may be high!). The worst situation occurs when a team takes pains to make a careful decision, and their recommendations are seemingly ignored. To truly collaborate, as we saw in Chapter 1, trust has to be high. It takes time to build trust, and it pays dividends to be very careful in the beginning. As trust levels grow, speed increases. So, here's the paradox: if you want your organization to be fast and agile, go slowly at first. This is even more important for complex challenges in which there is a high level of ambiguity. How you choose among options has a tremendous impact on that level of trust.

THE 2×2 MATRIX

We recommend an alternative way to make these kinds of decisions: the 2×2 *matrix*. The matrix preserves the fair and transparent advantage of the other methods discussed earlier. It also allows you to consider two criteria at the same time.

An example of a 2×2 matrix is shown in Figure 6.1. In this example, the decision to be made is where to locate a new school. The school board has identified three possible sites (A, B, and C). The criteria are the cost of construction (the sites are on different kinds of terrain) and the level of activity that would surround the new school (some are in neighborhoods, others are in more congested areas of the city; all things being equal, the board would like to site the school in a quieter area). Each of the five members of the school board makes their own evaluation of those factors and chooses a spot on the matrix for each location (so, there are $5 \times 3 = 15$ dots on the matrix). It wasn't obvious to the board what the right choice would be since there wasn't one site that was clearly

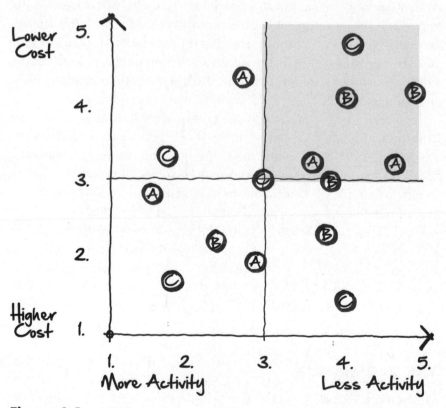

Figure 6.1 A 2×2 matrix.

both the quietest and the cheapest, but the matrix helps them visualize that there is, in fact, one choice that is probably optimal – Site B.

2×2 modeling is used in countless disciplines, because while it seems simple, it helps draw out more sophisticated thinking from a group. Having to consider two criteria at the same time forces people to see "both/and" potential, rather than "either/or." You naturally ask, "what if," to generate alternative views. It is a flexible and potent tool.

Using the Matrix

To use this tool, there is a very important decision to make: Which two criteria should be considered?

You could use any two criteria you decide are best-suited to your challenge, but we suggest two in particular: impact and ease of implementation (that's why we call it the *Big Easy*). You are looking for the opportunity that has the *largest* impact and is the *easiest* to implement. This sometimes seems counterintuitive to people. But stay with us.

Why these two criteria? Our experience is that selecting a first opportunity is critical to building the bonds of trust needed to move to the larger projects that will be needed for addressing complex challenges. You want people to be excited about what they are doing, and early success will keep them engaged for the long haul, drawing others in so that bigger opportunities are more achievable. As people build success by translating ideas into action, they are also building trust. As they are building trust, they are building the capacity to do more and more complex work together. Focusing on the Big Easy provides the right balance of a place to start.

The "Big" in the Big Easy inspires people and engages them emotionally. The "Easy" means that there are practical steps that can be taken now to move toward this opportunity. Taken together, these two dimensions ensure that the group has avoided two common risks: (1) selecting an idea that is very difficult to do and becoming discouraged, or (2) selecting something that is easy but inconsequential that no one will really care about.

If a team is working together for the first time, the chosen opportunity may indeed seem small and mundane. For example, we worked with a citywide group of citizens and leaders that was concerned

that their community was on the decline. A major concern was a
deteriorating downtown area – as in most cities, retail had moved out
to the suburbs leaving an empty feel on Main Street. After a one-day
off-site meeting about revitalizing the downtown, the team returned
with a beautification project for planters in downtown. The reaction
from those that had not been part of the session: "That's it?! All day to
decide to build planters?" In reality, the planters were just the first step
together, so the team could move to larger opportunities that involved
deeper commitments. The group went on to revitalize their ailing
downtown and found many ways to work together that would not have
been possible before.

As this example shows, even though the Big Easy may seem quite
small, resist the urge to go big. We've seen countless first projects like
those planters – small efforts that attract attention that in turn attract
more support. People generally want to join successful efforts, and that
brings a wider range of skills and resources to the project. The network for the opportunity expands and larger, more complex work can
be accomplished. People who once thought nothing could happen to
improve a neighborhood, downtown, business, or organization notice
the trend and want to lend their support to the project.

To understand why this happens, think back to our description of
different kinds of people in Chapter 1. If you're just starting out, you
probably have mostly pioneers around the table. The pragmatists are,
for the most part, hanging back to see whether this effort will have stay-
ing power and if they can trust the group to treat them and their time
well. If you pick an opportunity that is too ambitious and lose steam,
you'll never get the pragmatists to join you. Demonstrate success, however, even with a small undertaking and they will be much more likely
to throw their lot in with the group.

In some instances, a team's members may already know each other
well. However, poor habits may have deflated the team. Perhaps they
keep meeting with no decisions and no progress. Perhaps everyone
has their own project in mind. Or, worse still, cynicism has eroded
the will to do anything at all. The 2×2 matrix can help teams break
through old habits and show their opportunities in a new light. It can
rejuvenate a team around the potential for change and inspire others
to join.

DEALING WITH DOUBTS AND DOUBTERS

This way of choosing a direction may seem quite unscientific. In fact, it depends on the powerful idea of *group intuition*. When there is a complicated choice to be made, one individual may or may not know exactly how much impact an idea will have, or how easy it will be to pull it off. However, if a group of reasonably well-informed people all make individual judgments about the two dimensions of impact and ease, the combined weight of all of those judgments will lead the group in the right direction. In our experience, by using a 2×2 matrix to surface a shared strategic intuition, teams gain insights faster, learn faster, and act faster.

The odds are that the opportunity chosen really is your Big Easy. But what if you encounter doubters? Structuring your next steps in the same way that software developers do – taking baby steps to "try out" the Big Easy – is one way to respond to that worry. If the first steps toward your Big Easy opportunity prove that it was a dud, the group can easily go back and focus on another opportunity. This "try-out period" is an important advantage of agile strategy over traditional strategic planning. When months and thousands of dollars have been spent developing a strategic plan, it's very difficult to admit that some of the assumptions were wrong. With agile strategy, a limited amount of time will be "wasted" should the team be heading down what turns out to be a wrong path. Even if the group chooses the wrong opportunity to start, they will likely learn a lot from failure. If they quickly assess what's wrong and move on to another opportunity, chances are they have also strengthened habits of shared learning and candid communication. Facing hard facts together also builds trust. In this way, agile strategy enables you to manage risk in a way that traditional strategic planning never can.

Another common hesitation about using the Big Easy method is that it might appear to be premature to make any decision at all. That is, some members of the group may feel they need more information. But there is a real risk of delaying a decision on which opportunity to pursue. The group can become fixated on infinite fine tuning, ranking and reranking. Looking for more data can simply delay moving ideas into action. Because we are confronting complex, adaptive challenges, we must accept four realities. First, delay – too much talk without action – erodes trust. If getting more information is simply an excuse for not doing anything, the trust in your group will begin to evaporate. Second, it is impossible to have enough information to analyze a complex challenge completely before we begin. Third, we will only really learn about this complex challenge when we begin to do something together. We need to experiment and test our ideas. Fourth, you can be continuously both "generating" and "consuming" data by asking questions *as* you move forward. As you explore for answers, you will look for more data to guide you. We recommend you choose an opportunity that motivates the group to immediate action.

Sometimes it's tempting to combine opportunities to limit the scope of the choice – it feels safer than picking just one. However, we don't recommend this maneuver – the idea can get muddied and it's hard to tell if it is really a Big Easy. If the people making judgments are reasonably insightful, you can be confident that whatever you choose is probably very good.

Finally, you may find that what you chose as the Big Easy does not fit a progression that is in your (or someone else's) head for how the overall opportunity should come together. A debate may ensue about sequencing various ideas: What should come first? If the assets are in place to launch the Big Easy we recommend you move forward and not worry about the order. Given enthusiasm and desire for success, the team will find that once the first opportunity is accomplished, they can then move to the next opportunity and the order will address itself. Opportunities will connect over time, and the speed of your work will increase as your team grows. You'll also get better at spotting the next opportunity to take on.

PUTTING THE SKILL TO WORK: THE AGILE LEADER AS PRIORITIZER

Using the 2×2 matrix as a way to choose among different options is as simple as drawing a four-square grid on a piece of paper (if you're working in a group, draw a large matrix on a flip chart). Put one criterion along the bottom, and another along one side. Label the ends of each of these axes – one end is high, another low. Each person votes by indicating where on the matrix they think each idea falls (an easy way to do this is to use sticky dots; assign each idea a different color or put numbers on them). The opportunity that has the most votes in the quadrant that represents high ratings for both criteria is the "winner."

There are many ways that you can begin using the 2×2 matrix to help you to make choices. An interesting way to explore the idea is to practice finding the Big Easy in your own life. Make a list of projects at your house that you've been wanting to accomplish and evaluate them on the scale of impact and ease, or price and ease, or price and impact.

When you practice the Big Easy, you will find your skills for making choices improving. Agile leaders use these skills to help guide choices about which opportunities make the most sense, even when the environment is a complex one.

CASE STUDY: FINDING A WAY TO JUMP-START NEW ECONOMIC ACTIVITY

The southern Indiana region north of Louisville, Kentucky has a rich heritage of agriculture, which is still a dominant economic factor in many of its communities. In the early 1980s two different outlet malls were constructed along two different interchanges off Interstate I-65, which runs through the region. There was a good deal of excitement that these new malls would breathe new life into the economy. One mall took off and remains a regional shopping destination. The other, the smaller development of the two, never quite made the impact that leaders had hoped for. For years, the facility was greatly underutilized. Local leaders decided that a good repurposing of the facility might be in converting it to an agricultural distribution hub to better capitalize on the agriculture-related economy. Ground work and due diligence began. Months and then years went by without much headway.

Frustrated by the lack of progress, a different kind of conversation began to emerge – less about what the region didn't have (investment to convert the outlet mall) but instead what they did have. Scott was invited to be part of these new conversations through his role with Purdue's Cooperative Extension office. Cooperative extension is an initiative at land grant institutions designed to serve as the liaison between knowledge created at the university and application of those ideas in local communities.

The group realized that while repurposing the old outlet mall might indeed be a way to develop the agriculture-based economy, there might be other ways as well. Lots of ways, actually. One opportunity in particular emerged as a Big Easy, the potentially big idea that would be easy to implement – easier, it seemed, than the opportunity associated with the outlet mall.

The group was led by an IT entrepreneur named Tim Burton, who had begun a side business making maple syrup, tapping the trees on his land. The group began to consider the idea of having a maple syrup festival to help celebrate the agricultural heritage and perhaps provide an economic shot in the arm to the region. Other communities in Indiana also had maple syrup festivals, and the group initially assumed that the New England region of the United States surely had something of a monopoly on the maple syrup festival market. Through some research, however, the group learned that no community in the country had a *national* maple syrup festival. Tim and his friends quickly claimed Jackson County, and more specifically Medora, Indiana (population 697) as the home of the National Maple Syrup Festival.

The first national maple syrup festival was held 15 months later. Soon word began to spread and the annual festival began drawing thousands of visitors. Tim sold his IT business and began working full-time on maple syrup production and distribution, calling his new enterprise Burton's Maplewood Farms. Tiny Medora, Indiana now exports its syrup-related products across the United States. And, they are not just selling syrup as a commodity. Tim's business model includes partnering with regional distilleries to age his syrup in rum and whisky barrels, selling to many of the finest chefs in the United States and to customers through farmers' markets and gourmet food events around the country. And the festival? After a few years it had grown too large for tiny Medora to handle, so it was expanded to a regional festival extending to several southern Indiana counties.

Chapter 7

CONVERT YOUR IDEAS TO OUTCOMES WITH MEASURABLE CHARACTERISTICS (SKILL 6)

S ome of you are seriously considering skipping this entire chapter – the words "outcomes" and "measurable" don't sound like ideas you want to think about too much.

Keep reading and give us a chance to change your mind.

Here is the vision statement of a large organization that we came across recently (the names have been changed to protect the innocent):

Be the global leader in customer value.

This statement is frankly nothing more than a collection of words that say *nothing* about the core mission of the organization. What's worse, it probably took weeks or months to craft, and it's highly likely there was an expensive contract with a consultant to provide expert assistance.

We can laugh, but most of us have been on one of these kinds of groups. With the benefit of hindsight, we can't believe we were part of this kind of process. How did it happen? It starts with the best of intentions. You're at the first meeting of a new network or organization. Before long, someone says, "I know what we need – a vision statement." There's lots of head-nodding around the table – it's a concrete task after the initial meandering conversation. "Finally," each person says to themselves, "we've got some direction." Everyone eagerly dives in.

But after a while – sometimes not until several meetings have passed – the group finds itself *still* trying to find language that everyone accepts. They move from specific descriptive words to more general concepts. Before they know it, they've got a vision statement like the one above. And far too often, they don't really know what to do after they've "ratified" the vision.

With this skill, we're suggesting that you go about things very differently. There might be a time and place to create a vision statement for a brand-new organization, but in any other setting, don't kid yourselves: a vision statement is not going to help you get anything done. If you have a basic direction, that's good enough to move forward. Agile leaders know how to translate ideas into meaningful, measurable outcomes that, when pursued, will help organizations achieve their most cherished ideals.

91

GREAT IDEAS LIE BELOW THE SURFACE

If a vision statement won't get things moving, what should you do instead? Rather than watching the discussion get more and more general, agile leaders drive the conversation deeper. They don't go for vague feel-good adjectives and nouns. They help groups have the kinds of deep conversations that will allow them to explore what they are really hoping for and dreaming about in coming together.

Imagine you're designing a house with your partner. You're meeting with the architect, who asks you what you want the kitchen to look like. "I'd like it to look industrial," you say, "all professional-grade stainless steel appliances, black granite, that kind of thing." Your partner looks at you in horror. "I thought we'd agreed this would be like that place we rented by the lake last year . . . you know, 'glamping' (glamour + camping)! Lots of wood – cozy but luxurious!"

Fortunately, your architect has been through a lot of these kinds of projects. She's not going to let you head to divorce court over this kind of thing. She asks you a question you weren't expecting: "Tell me about the kinds of experiences you see happening in the kitchen if it's a fabulous room." You're both quiet for a moment, then your partner says, "There's really good food being cooked." "And good wine," you add. Then the ideas come quickly: there's music – maybe people will even start to dance. Loud laughter. People hang out there rather than going in the living room. It's easy for your friends who are parents to bring their kids to parties with them. You can clean up in only a few minutes. In fact, it's hard for you to *stop* talking about your wonderful new kitchen.

"Okay," the architect says. "Why don't you come back next week?" At your next meeting, she pulls out her laptop and has one of those programs that lets you walk around a virtual room. She has a kitchen on the screen, and she's put people in as well, who are obviously enjoying themselves. She uses the 360-degree feature to let you look all around the room. "Yes!" you both say. "That's what I was trying to describe last week."

The architect knows better than to point out what we, the invisible observers, have noticed: the kitchen doesn't look at all like what you described – no black granite countertops. And it doesn't look much like what your partner described, either – it's too big to ever be described as "cozy" and there's no rough-hewn wood in sight.

What just happened? Did you compromise? No. A compromise would have been rustic cabinets with lots of black granite, or industrial-grade appliances crammed into a small space. You *both* would have hated it. Did your architect deliver a "vision statement" kitchen – an empty room with just outlines so you'd know that it would, in fact, have cabinets and counters and appliances? That approach would only have postponed the argument to a later date.

What the architect did was to work from what you imagined a "successful" kitchen would be. She knew that in truth you weren't most concerned about the color of the counters, and the exact size wasn't the do-or-die item for your partner. What transcended all of those things is what you want to feel when you're in that room . . . you arrived at an agreement talking about very specific things that would happen there.

THREE QUESTIONS TO ASK

When we're helping groups adopt an agile strategy approach, we ask them to consider three questions:

1. If we are successful, what will we see?
2. What will we feel?
3. Whose lives will be different and how?

These questions are very qualitative by design. They ask you to imagine what something would be like and to describe it so that others can imagine it as well – the more specific, the better. This may feel uncomfortable, particularly if you're technically oriented and most attuned to data and charts and graphs. Try to suspend your discomfort and engage the more visual and creative parts of your brains. We often tell people to close their eyes for a few minutes of silence when they get to this point. Then we ask them to verbalize what they're imagining.

What is this "touchy-feely" stuff about? There's a technical word for what you're doing: *prospection*. The best way to describe prospection is that it is reminiscing . . . forward. When you reminisce, you're not just remembering *facts* about something in the past; for example,

"My grandmother was born in 1907, she lived in Minnesota." There is an emotional element to reminiscing: "I remember going to my grandmother's house and baking cookies with her." Physiologically, when you reminisce your brain is releasing dopamine into your bloodstream – the same chemical that's behind the jolt of pleasure people get from addictive drugs like amphetamines. Likewise, prospection, in which you imagine a successful future (rather than the past), provides that same release of dopamine. You become emotionally invested in success. And *emotion* – not vague vision statements – is what drives people to action.

When you put this skill into action, a couple of things will happen. First, the idea itself will begin to change. You'll go from the fuzzy image on a black and white TV (remember those?) to high-definition. To illustrate what we mean, imagine a group working on school improvement. They've decided that their goal is *to improve the learning experience for middle school students*. Everyone can probably give general agreement to that idea. But it's still pretty fuzzy: Are they talking about rewriting curriculum? Changing the physical space in the classrooms? Upgrading the teachers' skills? Every person in the room could think that this is a quite specific goal and yet have a completely different set of assumptions about its meaning.

When they ask themselves the questions we suggest earlier, here's their revised draft:

> All our students will come running off their buses and into the school in the morning because they are so excited about the learning experience they know they'll have.
>
> We will feel great pride in our school – we will have educational leaders from around the state coming to visit because we've been recognized as an excellent school.
>
> Our students will be prepared to take the most challenging curriculum available in high school so they can follow their career aspirations.

Do you see the change? It might not be exactly what everyone had in mind originally, but when someone describes what they think success would be like in this way, others can feel that it's right. People say things like, "Yes, you've captured it – I was thinking about something a little different, but you've really put your finger on it."

Embedded in the group's statements is a future they would each like to see: they want their students to be highly engaged in the learning process, and for that to result in high achievement. As members share their ideas, the idea may continue to become more concrete as new dimensions are uncovered. Imagine one member of the group speaks up:

> I think we're missing something. Here's what I said for the "whose lives will be different?" question: We will have teachers from throughout the country clamoring to work at our school because they have the freedom to be excellent rather than having to "teach to the test." Aren't we trying to get away from the constant testing?

This statement introduces a new element, and the conversation deepens to sort it out – are they talking about college preparation, or about standardized testing? In using this skill, the agile leader needs to keep driving down until they reach those deepest shared aspirations and dreams. The group might refine their first statement a bit to incorporate the new idea:

> All our students come running off their buses and into the school in the morning because they are so excited about the learning experience that awaits them – it's based on exploring ideas, not preparing for a test.

One important thing that will happen when you apply this skill is that each person will emotionally engage with the outcome. If you had functional MRI scanners like the ones in brain research labs, you'd see the dopamine coursing through the members' bloodstreams! The group is no longer a task force they're on, it's something they are personally committed to. People start to physically lean in, to gesture. They are seeing the outcome "in their mind's eye." For real transformation (in any area), you will need that engagement, that commitment. When you see this body language, you know you're on the right track.

MEASURING

We all see things from our own perspective. A tree might be described as gigantic by someone from the desert, while someone who grew up around redwoods might say it was on the short side. If the two meet and describe the tree to one another, you can bet that their descriptions will be very different indeed. If these two people are to have a productive conversation, they need a way to talk about the tree that doesn't rely on their own experiences. The only ways to accurately convey the size of the tree are to either measure it directly, or to compare it to something that both people have seen.

Many of us dislike metrics because they're so often used as statements of success or failure or as a means of control. This skill invites us to think about metrics in a different way: metrics are a way to develop a common language, so that we know we are talking about the same thing. If you can get to agreement about how you would measure a successful outcome, you can be fairly sure that you are aligned toward the same outcome. For example, the outcome statement about students being excited to get to school each morning might be measured by (among other things) tracking absenteeism.

The other reason that metrics are unpopular is that data can be arduous to gather with any precision. You might have to buy new equipment, train others to take measurements, learn the software to analyze the data, or get approval to launch a survey. It might even mean hiring new staff or an external evaluator, just to make sure it's done right and in compliance with laws or a funder's requirements. No wonder we inwardly groan when we hear the word!

You'll be relieved to learn that for our purposes, selecting the ways in which you might measure an outcome does *not* necessarily mean that you're pledging to actually carrying out the measuring. You might do so . . . or you might not. You are not writing an assessment or evaluation plan or committing to Key Performance Indicators. *For now*, you are only using this skill as a way to engage and align a group's members toward a shared outcome. You have the freedom to think expansively about what success would look like – if a longitudinal (and very expensive) series of focus groups with users would be the best way to measure whether a project, product or service has achieved the original aims, choose that as a way to measure. Or, maybe you select something simple and intuitive. The point we underscore is this: to get alignment within a group, you need to define a shared outcome that everyone can see in their mind's eye. You need to drive your conversation deeper with enough specificity that you can come up with metrics. When you start describing the future with metrics you have passed the threshold of vague language. You are now communicating with each other with enough clarity that people can "see" what the others are thinking. You are achieving alignment toward an outcome. This use of metrics stands apart from formal assessment. Of course, assessment is important, and you may decide that the measures you identify form the building blocks of an evaluation plan – but that should be a separate decision.

To go back to the school example, the participants might agree that absenteeism would be one good way to measure that "running off the bus" kind of student engagement. Now, they can be fairly confident that they have converged on what engagement means. Let's look at what can happen if a group decides to skip the conversation about what success would mean and possible accompanying metrics. When you stick to general vision statements (even if *you* don't think they're that general), you may find yourself a few weeks or months later facing angry disagreements: "What?! I thought we were doing 'this,' not 'that'!" One person might think student engagement means that students will be completing their homework assignments. Another person might think that student engagement means the amount of time students spend on extracurricular activities. The point is this: the term "engagement" is too vague for us to ensure alignment. We need to go deeper and describe the future we want to create. We need to describe what people will be seeing, feeling, and doing.

Less obviously, without a deeper conversation people may decide they don't really have time for "yet another committee." They will vote with their feet and exit the scene. They don't disagree with the vision statement, but it never captured their imagination, either. Often, not much has happened beyond the vision statement – the group still isn't sure what it should *do*. For the pragmatists in the group, other more pressing demands have led them to decide that they just can't get involved with this initiative. You've wasted time and, more importantly, the participants' trust of one another.

In some ways this skill is the most counterintuitive of the ten in this book. It's easy to think that any quick agreement on fairly general goals – even a vaguely worded vision statement – is a positive thing. As we began to write this chapter, Ed shared a story from his work in China. During the 1990s he negotiated a number of joint venture agreements for his clients. His Chinese colleague, a former intelligence officer for the Chinese government, had a great deal of experience watching how US managers negotiated with their Chinese partners. He suggested that US managers are often too quick to jump to a signing a contract without having a deeper understanding of shared outcomes: precisely how mutual benefits will be generated. Ed's Chinese colleague even had an expression that captured what happens when partners do not fully understand where they want to go together. Problems will inevitably arise because the partners end up "sleeping in the same bed but dreaming different dreams."

So, while it's tempting to move forward on a somewhat vague, our experience is the same as Ed's Chinese colleague, and not just where international joint ventures are concerned. Vagueness tends to doom the work from the start. The words do not emotionally engage people, and without emotion, people do not move. You may fear that deeper conversation will trigger dissension and arguments. But agile leaders know that just the opposite happens. We can overcome apathy with clarity and specificity, and we prevent future dissension by having a more sophisticated conversation now. Agile leaders who take this step reap great benefits as the group continues its work together, more committed than ever to making sure their efforts succeed.

PUTTING THE SKILL TO WORK: THE AGILE LEADER AS DREAMCATCHER

In using this skill, the agile leader is helping the group articulate its dreams and then make them tangible enough to pursue. As you might have guessed, the place to start is to ask the three questions: What would we see? What would we feel? Whose life would be different and how? Leave time for a substantive and somewhat meandering conversation – although it probably won't take as long as some conversations about vision statements!

Try for at least three statements about the outcome – not necessarily one answer to each of the questions (sometimes one or more of the questions just doesn't connect for a particular concept), but three or four statements in all. It's tempting to just take a vote on the most popular statements and move on. Resist that temptation, and let it take as much time as is needed, within reason, to find the ones that really resonate – in our experience, between 20 and 40 minutes is about right.

Once you have statements about what a successful outcome would look like, go back to each one and name a couple of ways you could measure that quality. Remember, you're not (yet) committing to *doing* the measurement – at this stage, you're just trying to make sure that you each understand the outcome in the same way. For now, you have the freedom to propose a costly longitudinal study or an expensive tracking system (of course, before you actually launch a project, you'll want to return to the conversation about how to monitor progress and assess outcomes).

It is only when we are sure of what we want – in detail – that we can really pursue it. This skill allows agile leaders to guide groups in the kind of dialogue that is needed in order to come to a shared commitment to a common destination. With a clear picture of success and how it could be measured, the group is ready to consider the actions that will produce that success.

CASE STUDY: USING METRICS TO SPUR NEW WORKFORCE DEVELOPMENT STRATEGIES IN KOKOMO

A casualty of increasing globalization in manufacturing was Delphi Automotive's decision to cut 600 jobs in Kokomo, Indiana. Delphi had been part of the General Motors family, with 200,000 employees worldwide creating electronics for GM's automobile manufacturing operations. In 2005, the company filed for bankruptcy. In Kokomo, the layoffs hit engineers and technologists particularly hard – high-paying jobs whose loss caused a tremendous negative ripple effect in surrounding north central Indiana. Reeling from the announcement, local leaders eagerly signed on to partner with Purdue University to apply for a $15 million US Department of Labor Workforce Innovation in Regional Economic Development (WIRED) grant. The application proposed efforts in a 12-county region, with Kokomo at the center. When word came from Washington that the application had been successful, Scott convened representatives from more than 100 regional organizations for conversations about how to prepare a regional workforce for a twenty-first-century economy. A set of civic forums was organized to explore four focus areas: talent development, entrepreneurship, civic leadership, and economic cluster expansion.

We gave you a preview of this project in the introduction of the book, but now we'd like to explain exactly how the initiative achieved its remarkable results. The Purdue team treated the grant much like venture capitalists would: about three-quarters of the money was used for an opportunity fund that would incentivize groups of people to address specific targets established by the Department of Labor. As the team considered how to structure the process, they thought about what success would look like. One criterion rose to the top: only ideas that included collaborations across organizations and counties would be funded. They also asked their partners – the groups that were asking for funding – to establish their own measures of success (about 200 metrics in all, over the course of the project). Funds were made available in stages, with small amounts of funding for exploratory work.

The initial forums surfaced ideas for the exploratory grants – about 60 experiments in how to build a modern regional workforce. Some experiments worked; others did not. The successful ideas were scaled up, with additional funding for demonstration projects, and larger amounts still for full implementation. Throughout the process, the Purdue team tracked progress against the measures from both the Department of Labor and the goals that project teams had set for themselves.

This outcome-focused perspective paid off in several ways. First, because of the attention to data collection, at the end of the project the Purdue team was able to demonstrate that they outpaced their proposed goals three times over. Second, the way in which funding was distributed, with additional funding only made available when there was evidence of success, was very effective: although the Indiana WIRED grant constituted only 8% of all the money awarded nationally under the program, the results accounted for 40% of the progress toward the national WIRED goals. And finally, the team's insistence on collaboration helped ensure sustainability for the many initiatives: two years after the grant ended, 80% of the initiatives were still active.

Delphi is back, although with a new name (Delphi Technologies) and a smaller footprint, with a few hundred employees focused on emerging opportunities in the hybrid automobile and other markets. Kokomo, too, is back: in 2014 it was named one of the top ten fastest-growing cities in America – a testament to the power of collaboration.

Chapter 8

START SLOWLY TO GO FAST – BUT START (SKILL 7)

I magine, for a moment, that you are standing on a beach gazing out at a distant island. Your kayak sits next to you. You are planning a day trip to the island and back, and you're getting a bit of a late start; you have to make sure you'll be back by sundown.

You face a choice. You could sit on the beach and try to plan your trip in detail to make sure it will be successful. To do that, you'd have to take measurements of the strength of the wind and its direction. You would calculate the size and direction of the waves. You would have to check the weather to see if the winds are likely to pick up or calm down. You need to estimate the timing of the tides and the strength of the pull of the moon. You would also have to remind yourself to estimate the impact of currents on your course. With all this information, you would then need to make some calculations to plot your course.

Alternatively, you could check the weather forecast, quickly assess the conditions ahead of you, get in the water, and start paddling.

The smart choice is to pick up that paddle. The only way to understand the true impact of the wind and the waves on our kayak is to experience it. We can then make calculations on the fly and adjust. Using the same approach, we can see how the other invisible factors influence the direction of our kayak. We don't really need to know whether it's the tides or the current that are causing our boat to drift. We simply see that our boat is drifting, and we make a subtle change in our direction. On a calm day, we don't need to make these adjustments very frequently. But if the wind were to pick up so that the wave action on our boat were to become more violent, we would be smart to make these adjustments more frequently. Instead of adjusting our course every ten minutes or so, we might make adjustments after only two or three paddle strokes.

We like this kayaking analogy because it captures a lot of the uncertainty that we all face as we live our lives. We may all have an outcome to achieve in our mind – a better job, a more agile organization, a more prosperous community – and we want to get there as quickly as we can. The reality is that we really can't learn how to make progress toward that outcome until we start *doing* something. That does not mean that we don't sit for a moment, gather some information (like a weather report), and think. It does, however, mean that we don't try to come up with the perfect plan. We don't become paralyzed with analysis. We don't lock down our capacity to act by engaging our fears. Instead, we face the future with confidence in our ability to experience what we can't fully understand, to learn, and to make decisions that blend both facts and our intuition. We have enough experience to recognize that we can trust our intuition, yet we are smart enough to realize that we might be wrong. We might need to make adjustments. When the invisible forces affecting our course are strong and quickly changing, we will need to be prepared to make some quick decisions.

The agile leader understands the limits of our capacity to understand and analyze complex, invisible systems. Agile leaders are biased toward action for a simple reason: we only learn about these complex systems by doing. If we want to make big changes fast, we have to go slow … but above all, we have to *go*.

LAUNCHING YOUR LEARNING

When you have an outcome in your mind, it does not have to be perfect to start. Equally important, you don't need to plot a perfect path to your outcome before you do anything. In order to learn how to get from here (where you stand) to there (the outcome you want), you need to start. You start with something quite limited in scope – the first few paddle strokes, so to speak – and see what happens.

Here's why: without starting, you can easily become overwhelmed. Karl Weick, a psychologist at Cornell University, published an important paper in 1984 that captured this idea. Weick was exploring why large-scale social problems can close down innovation. These social problems, such as increasing poverty, rising crime rates, environmental pollution, heart disease, or traffic congestion can loom so large in our minds that we become paralyzed. Sensationalizing these problems, all in the hope of mobilizing action, can do just the opposite. We easily become more frustrated, and we are more prone to feeling helpless. Weick astutely observes, "Ironically, people often can't solve problems, unless they think they aren't problems." He proposes the idea of addressing the challenges of large problems with an approach emphasizing the value of "small wins."

We've all been in those situations, in which we've defined a problem at such a large scale and general terms that we have no idea where to start. "Boiling the ocean" is a bit of somewhat-annoying business jargon that captures the idea. We can never boil the ocean simply because there is too much water. In the same vein, we can never make much progress, if we set ourselves up with an impossible task from the start. We are taking on more than we can handle. Because our resources are limited, we end up spreading ourselves too thin. We end up, as Weick observes, feeling frustrated and helpless. By contrast, when we break big challenges into smaller, more manageable tasks, we not only reduce our risks, we also increase the chance of feeling good about getting something accomplished.

Weick's ideas have taken hold, especially in the worlds of design and innovation. Elizabeth Gerber, a professor of design at Northwestern University, highlights the importance of *low fidelity prototyping*, a closely related idea. Gerber defines a low-fidelity prototype as a minimally detailed expression of an idea. In the case of designing a new website, a low-fidelity prototype might simply be a drawing. For a new product, it might be a cardboard mock-up. According to Gerber, low fidelity prototyping speeds up the development process. She cites a number of reasons: it reframes the possibility of failure into an opportunity for learning; it improves communication among team members; it provides the team with a sense of progress; and it increases a team's confidence in their own creativity.

There's another reason that getting projects off the ground quickly is important. They act as experiments to test some key assumptions. In the management world, good experiments help companies deal with complex, dynamic situations. Perfect knowledge is not possible, so the best option involves testing ideas. Jeanne Liedtka, professor at the Darden School of Business at the University of Virginia, calls these experiments *learning launches*. This concept captures the entrepreneurial mind-set and the bias toward action. Analysis can be time-consuming, misleading and paralyzing (think of the poor soul trying to analyze every detail of a kayak trip). In contrast, designing experiments generates knowledge about what works (or doesn't). This practical knowledge is far more immediate and relevant than a grand plan.

QUALITIES OF A GOOD STARTING PROJECT

We've concluded that there are a number of important characteristics of a good starting project:

They are short (enough): As with group size (p. 51), they follow the "Goldilocks Rule" – not so simple that they can be completed in a week, but not so complex that they take a year to complete. If the project is too short, you won't have enough time to reap the other benefits that we'll describe in a moment. If the project takes too long, your team can easily get bogged down and discouraged; 90 to 120 days is a good length to avoid both of these risks.

They engage everyone on the team: They build trust among team members, but this can't happen if only part of the team is involved. This usually happens for two reasons: First, the idea may be too simple. If it is *too* easy the group will lose interest early and could disband before the more difficult work is addressed. What's too easy? As long as the idea will take at least a small contribution from everyone, it's big enough. Remember the planters the citizen's downtown improvement group wanted to build? Although it's straightforward, there was plenty to do: pick locations, get permissions, buy materials, assemble the planters, and make a plan for ongoing maintenance. There is another bad habit we are trying to overcome with this idea. Many of us are in the habit of coming up with good ideas for *someone else* to do. This tendency works against the formation of a cohesive team. You can't outsource this process.

They create a "buzz," garnering attention for the work: They present a wonderful opportunity to create a new story, a new narrative, about what is possible through collaboration. Every organization and community has a narrative. Too often these narratives look backward. They are often cynical. A good starting project provides a new narrative to explain what is possible if we align our efforts and adopt new ways of thinking and behaving. The team provides a model to follow.

They test some key assumptions: At the early stages of a collaboration, we are making some key assumptions. An early project enables us to test some of these assumptions and accumulate new insights. For example, a low-fidelity prototype often tests customer acceptance: Will customers be willing to pay for the product, and how much? A Chamber of Commerce hosts an afterwork event downtown. Will this idea draw enough people to launch something like a "First Fridays" series? A company wants to retain its young talent. Will more professional development opportunities help?

They don't require permission: It's important to work on a project that can start immediately. That is, the team designing the project does not need permission to launch it. It is important to move a potential collaboration out of the talking stage quickly. Otherwise, the probability of success declines dramatically. Team members lose focus and enthusiasm when permission becomes an obstacle – you suddenly find yourself back in "If Only Land." Avoid this by designing a starting project that does not require permission. You are better off scaling back a project than designing one that can be easily delayed or derailed.

KEEPING THE TEAM ON TRACK

A starting project does not need a detailed project plan with milestones. However, it does need a logical route to follow, and it's useful to mark the path with *guideposts* – just a few key points along the way that will warn you if you're getting off course. In this way, guideposts help a team manage risks. Much like walking a trail, the team knows that if it misses a guidepost, it should stop and figure out why. Should they reset their course? Is the project too ambitious? Has a key assumption failed? Deciding on what the guideposts are should be also confirms that you'll be able to complete the project in a reasonable time. Remember, you are using your project as a learning process to figure out what works.

Here's an example from our work. Suppose a corporate team comes together to design a new approach to managing customer relationships The company has multiple divisions, each selling a different product line – primarily business office equipment and furniture. Some, but not all, of these business units have customers in common. Originally the divisions were separate companies, and over the years, various mergers and acquisitions have resulted in a single company. However, each division has its own sales operations, and each of those uses its own "customer relationship management" (CRM) software platform. A CRM includes all the relevant data about each customer – contact information, sales history, deals being negotiated. These CRMs do not communicate with one another, so if a customer from one division decides to buy a product from a salesperson representing a different division, that salesperson has to enter all of the same information over again in the new CRM, process a new credit application, and so on. This is a huge waste of time for both company employees and customers. The company's upper management team defines an outcome of deploying a new single CRM across the company over the next two years. This system would include the capacity to analyze data to identify new cross-division sales opportunities as well as to flag problematic customers who take an inordinate amount of support or who do not pay on time. It would be a big shift for the company with a great deal of training required, but one the team is convinced will pay off handsomely in higher productivity.

The team defines their starting project as combining just a sample from two divisions' CRMs as a pilot. They reason that by installing this system on a small scale first, they can spot problems that might crop up before they launch a larger scale deployment. The team decides that the project will be up and running in 180 days. If all goes well, they will then integrate the two divisions' data into one CRM that could be expanded to other divisions. To set the guideposts for the project, the team then decides what has to be done in 45 days, 90, and 150 days, if they are to stay on track. So, for example, within 45 days, the team agrees it must decide on an outside vendor to help design the pilot and complete the specifications for a deployment that could scale across the entire company. In 90 days, all the test data needs to be uploaded. In 150 days, the training process for the sales team should be developed and approved.

WHAT NEXT?

Those first tentative paddle strokes will give you important information, but it wouldn't make for a very satisfying day on the ocean if you stopped there. It's best to think of our initial project as both standing alone and at the same time part of a series – when one is complete (or nearing completion), you'll see what the next one should be. You'll know what adjustments to make based on what you've learned, and possibly have identified some challenges you still need to learn more about. And while the kayak may be strictly a one-person craft, there is plenty of room for others to join you in pursing the goal you've set for yourself. That "buzz" you created means that you now have a bigger team and your next project can be bigger in scope.

Here's another example of this skill in action: a team of HR leaders has come together to think about its management training program. The company's current program targets "up and coming" young talent. Participants attend a series of weekend courses over the course of two years; at the end they have earned about half the credits needed for an MBA degree through a local university; many then choose to complete that degree on their own. The number and quality of applicants has decreased over the past few years, primarily because supervisors have to "nominate" participants and agree to pay about half the tuition cost – and the "word on the street" is that the program isn't worth it (and more generally, the MBA degree isn't in as much demand as when the program started more than 20 years ago). The team would like to create a set of courses based on simulations and other more modern learning approaches. They know that eventually the company's "top brass" will have to approve the new program, but several of those individuals came through the current traditional program and view it very favorably.

The team decides that these kinds of major changes in the curriculum will never happen without strong support throughout the company – beyond just the HR department. The team decides to test the assumption that this support can be galvanized. They design an initial project of creating a class that uses a "pop-up" format. Pop-ups are informal, noncredit classes that "pop up" informally for just a few sessions, and they are a great way to test student interest in a topic quickly. They hope a dozen or so participants will come to a one-session workshop on creating budgets – a modest goal, since it's scheduled for a weekday night, and they're not offering any food or drink. To their delight, more than forty employees show up. Not only have they demonstrated that there is plenty of interest, a few of the participants attending ask if they can be part of the re-design effort. Their next project, with an expanded team that can handle a bigger challenge: a series of pop-ups.

PUTTING THE SKILL TO WORK: THE AGILE LEADER AS EXPERIMENTER

Applying this skill means reminding yourself of where you want to go, and then finding a way in which you can start in a low-risk, small-scale way. Examples of good starting projects include projects like a pilot, a low fidelity prototype, a forum series, a website, site visits or field trips, customer discovery interviews, or a business plan (or a business model canvas). Remember that you are experimenting: you may find that your first project doesn't go the way you're hoping. That doesn't mean it's not the right project.

Agile leaders understand that especially in a complex environment with an adaptive challenge, moving toward a big goal requires experimentation and small steps. To go fast, one has to start by going slowly. Getting to a clearly defined starting project is an exciting moment for a group: chances are no one has traveled the exact path that the team has outlined. By quickly and confidently outlining a project with a handful of guideposts, the team is inviting others to contribute. The anticipation created by a good initial project is infectious. As an agile leader moves the project into action, the excitement will only grow.

CASE STUDY: OVERCOMING THE ACADEMIC BUREAUCRACY WITH SMALL WINS

A National Science Foundation grant to establish a National Center for Engineering Pathways to Innovation (Epicenter) was awarded in 2011 to Stanford University and VentureWell, a non-profit organization that furthers innovation and entrepreneurship in higher education. The mission of Epicenter was "to empower US undergraduate engineering students to bring their ideas to life." One key premise of the initiative was working with faculty to redesign the undergraduate engineering experience. The leaders of the initiative wanted to involve 50 higher education institutions, with the idea that 50 was a large enough number of institutions to achieve a "tipping point" in reimagining engineering education.

Before she joined the Purdue team, Liz was hired by VentureWell after the grant had been awarded to help lead the project. She quickly learned that while there was not yet a specific plan for how to effectively engage engineering faculty from 50 institutions, it was clear they needed to move swiftly to get results in the time remaining on the grant. She asked Ed and Scott to help her guide the faculty in using the principles of Strategic Doing.

Curricular change was a particular focus for the NSF, but the traditional concept of redesigning curriculum usually means new courses, which tend to get caught in the "bureaucratic buzzsaw" at many institutions. The arduous process of gaining approval often saps the energy of a group, even if the course is ultimately approved. To address this risk, the Epicenter team expanded the idea of change to encompass learning experiences more generally – whether or not those experiences happened in the context of a new course. Working in teams of three to eight people, the schools each identified one small starting project that might lead to bigger opportunities. The ideas were modest; for example, a new learning module for a course one of the members was teaching, a small "makerspace" with a few 3-D printers, or a competition in which students could propose innovative products or services they wanted to launch. But importantly, each was an idea that could be completed relatively quickly and did not need to go through an approval process. Liz followed up with the teams to help them stay on track and as they got the first project underway, encouraged them to pick a next small project.

Over a little less than three years, more than 500 such projects were launched, with as many as 31 by a single university. Many of these projects were fairly modest taken on their own. However, some were much bigger: the experience of success in taking on a small starting project helped the teams gain confidence in their ability to work together, and signaled to university leadership that theirs was a group that could "get things done." These completed projects often opened the way to new resources and institutional support and made possible major achievements at many of the schools, such as a new certificate program in entrepreneurship or even a new university center.

Chapter 9

DRAFT SHORT-TERM ACTION PLANS THAT INCLUDE EVERYONE (SKILL 8)

M any of us have been part of a great team at one point or another. If not, perhaps we've witnessed a great team in action. Often, a great team achieves their level of greatness after many hours of working together – the sports team made up primarily of seniors who have played together since freshman year, for instance. Or, your favorite comedy team that has performed together so long they can literally complete one another's thoughts. At work, we may know a small group of competent professionals that can seemingly tackle any problem, working together like a well-oiled machine.

What happens, however, when a group of people comes together for the first time and they don't have four years of practices and games to learn to work together, or even the luxury of a few months to work out the kinks? Is there any way to be highly productive beginning on Day 1? You may remember Amy Edmondson, who we encountered in Chapter 2 with the important idea of psychological safety. She sees this psychological safety as one of the key aspects of what she calls "teaming." She contends that when individuals follow the same set of guidelines or rules, they can begin functioning as a highly productive team immediately. She calls this teaming rather than teamwork.

Agile leadership means ensuring that good ideas don't die on the vine, by making sure that each member of a group shares the responsibility for implementation. Each person may have a different kind of task to move the idea forward, but there are no spectators. Agile leaders keep the expectations for any individual person small, knowing that modest commitments gathered together add up to significant progress.

SHARED LEADERSHIP

Great teams need great leaders, right? Well, yes and no. To explore this question further, let's focus on the term "leadership." When you hear the word "leader," who springs to mind? Maybe you envision a political or military figure, one living or one from history. Or, you may recall someone from the world of sports – a coach, perhaps. Others will think of a person much closer to home, someone who has touched their lives directly: a boss, a minister, or maybe a parent. Each of us will likely imagine someone different, with varied leadership characteristics and attributes; but most of us will be thinking about leadership as a quality that resides in a *single* person.

There have been many different single-person models of leadership taught in graduate programs and written about in the books that line our shelves. Ken Blanchard and Paul Hersey told us about "situational leadership." Robert Greenleaf helped us understand "the servant leader" and Jim Collins wrote about "five levels of leadership." All are different ways of thinking about leadership; all are based on the notion of the individual leader.

There is an evolution afoot in our thinking about leadership, one that doesn't focus on the individual; but, rather, on leadership as a *shared characteristic* of a group or a team. Shared leadership can give us flexibility in our groups and organizations when we are working on complex, strategic issues. We need others to join us in leadership to take on complex challenges.

Business educator and executive coach Marshall Goldsmith suggests that shared leadership is a way to maximize talent because it allows us to mix and match the best of individuals' leadership abilities to meet the complex challenges we face. He offers seven guidelines for fostering an organizational culture of shared leadership:

1. Give power away to individuals to allow them to strengthen their abilities.
2. Define clear boundaries for the decisions they are empowered to make.
3. Cultivate an organizational culture in which people feel able to take the initiative.
4. Give people the discretion and autonomy they need to complete tasks and deploy their resources.
5. Don't second guess the decisions of those who have been asked to make them.
6. Managers should consider themselves a resource rather than a supervisor.
7. Set up an agile, iterative processes that allows for regular check-ins to review progress and make adjustments if necessary. (Adapted from Goldsmith 2010)

It's very likely that the next iteration of the great individual leader will be the leader who designs teams and organizations in which the leadership is shared, creating the capacity needed to manage the complex issues we face.

ACTION PLANS FOR SHARED LEADERSHIP

Perhaps the most visible, pragmatic example of shared leadership is a shared action plan. The plan needs to be documented in writing, not just left to people's powers of recollection. A Chinese proverb expresses it this way: "The palest ink is better than the best memory." If you don't capture the conversation and put it into a form that can be easily retrieved later, the thinking and the agreements can be lost. An action plan lays out in detail what needs to happen next to keep moving forward.

In an action plan, members of the group take responsibility for the specific "to-do's" that need to be done. We suggest that an action plan be limited to a short timeframe – say, the next 30 days. Why? Because if you're in a complex environment, things change rapidly. As in the kayaking example in the last chapter, time spent planning too far out is very likely wasted time.

MICRO-COMMITMENTS BUILD TRUST

An action plan is really a promise, a promise that words will match actions. Promises kept, even small promises, result in increased trust. Donald Sull and Charles Spinosa refer to this as *promise-based management*. According to Sull and Spinosa, one of the reasons organizations face difficulty in strategy execution is the inability to develop clear commitments in a systematic way. This weakness is a function of the inability of leaders to build trust across an organization or a community.

We've discussed the notion of trust several times in this book. Promises, of course, are all about trust. Much has been written about the role of trust in teams and organizations. Suffice it to say that trust is critical to getting anything done together – much less the kinds of complex, adaptive challenges that many of us are struggling to confront. But how do you build trust at scale? One of the ways you do it is to ask for what we have come to call *micro-commitments*. The effectiveness of micro-commitments has been written about a good deal in the context of individual behavior. A significant retirement nest egg can be accumulated through small commitments of savings and investing over time. Health professionals know that big lifestyle changes to diet and exercise are nearly impossible, but smaller, incremental commitments tend to be more easily followed. Marla Cilley, better known as "FlyLady," gained prominence a few years ago for her system of conquering household management, 15 minutes at a time. Likewise, when we mentor doctoral students through their dissertation process we always suggest following the advice of Joan Bolker in her book, *Writing Your Dissertation in Fifteen Minutes a Day: A Guide to Starting, Revising, and Finishing Your Doctoral Thesis.*

Strategic conversations like the ones we've described in this book often result in actions that are in addition to what group members are doing on top of their regular job and/or life responsibilities. They're not in a position to commit hours to a new project – nor, at the beginning, do they trust the other members of the group enough to want to do so. We've found that micro-commitments have a remarkable impact in these kinds of groups and teams. The agile leader asks for micro-commitments, at least at first. We've noticed that group members' commitments will likely get progressively less "micro" as the group moves forward and sees progress being made, and members' trust in one another grows. Remember, our definition of trust is this: trust occurs when words match actions. Asking for micro-commitments provides the mechanism for that to happen.

Shared action plans can move groups and teams into action immediately. Leonard Schlesinger, the former president of Babson College, sees the ability to take immediate action as vital in a world in which you can no longer plan or predict your way to success. Along with co-author Charles Kiefer, Schlesinger makes several observations about the value of "doing" immediately. Doing allows us to quickly learn what works and what doesn't. If we never do, we will never know what is possible and what is not. Doing leads to reactions, which can lead us in other, sometimes unexpected directions. As we do, we will find people to come along side with us. And finally, doing will always lead us to evidence.

While it sometimes seems that the do-ers are in short supply, in fact there are many people who would rather do than talk. To return once again to the bell curve in Chapter 1, with the pioneers and the sore-heads on either end, these are the many pragmatists in the middle of the curve. *Most* people want to do, not just talk. One of our colleagues in Flint has what she calls a "two-meeting rule." When she is invited to meetings, she has a simple litmus test as to whether the meeting is worth her time – whether she walks away with a task to do. She says she may let one non-action-oriented meeting slide; but if she's asked to attend another of that group and there is no action being taken, she will not meet with that group a third time. That violates her two-meeting rule.

Agile leaders like our colleague in Flint want to do things, not just talk about things. They understand the need for action undertaken by a group, in which each person understands that they share leadership toward the common goal.

PUTTING THE SKILL TO WORK: THE AGILE LEADER AS DEAL-CLOSER

While the action plan is straightforward, it's also easy for this step to go awry if careful attention isn't paid to the details. Each person should have something to do in the action plan – a promise they are making to the group. Sull and Spinosa suggest several attributes for good trust-enhancing promises: they are public, voluntary, active, and specific. We've made that list a bit more concrete; when you're developing an action plan, you want to include everything that needs to happen in the next 30 days, and for each item you should specify:

Who: This sounds simple enough, but it does not always get accomplished the way it should. A specific name (or at most, two names) should be assigned to each item. "Everyone" too often means "no one."

What: This should also be specific. What is it that the person will be doing? For example, making three phone calls to whom? Writing up what? Going to look at what?

Deliverable: Each action item should also have a clear deliverable. Often it is a written document of some sort. If someone is talking to three people about a topic, the deliverable might be a paragraph about what they learned, distributed to other team members.

By When: Again, this should be a specific day. It could be tomorrow, it could be next week. If this is a 30-day action plan, then all action items should be completed within 30 days. When possible, avoid an action plan in which all items are due at the last minute – stagger the work so that it happens over the time period.

Even though this kind of plan is all about shared leadership, an agile leader takes responsibility for putting it together. We suggest going person to person, asking for their commitment, calling each by name and making eye contact: "Javier, what can you do? Mary, what can you do? Bill, what about you, what can you do with an hour of your time over the next 30 days?" Everyone should leave the meeting with something to do. The only exception would be truly major life events or urgent professional responsibilities that are temporary in nature: a member is having a baby, is in charge of a national conference, and so on. In addition, while it's fine for someone to indicate that someone on their staff will *help* them with a task, their commitment of time should be their own. After the meeting, make sure that the plan is disseminated back to the group members quickly, within 24 hours if possible.

Why an hour? We've found that it's a good standard for a micro-commitment. If each person spends one hour a month on the action plan, that is enough to generate significant progress. When five to seven people take individual small steps, collectively they take a large step. It is also small enough that it is difficult for people to say "No."

Agile leaders know how to help a group move from talk to doing with commitments to take action. Agile leaders are not afraid to call on each member of the group to make at least a small commitment of time, understanding that these commitments, when taken together, help move the group forward, build trust, and illuminate the path ahead.

CASE STUDY: TAKING COLLECTIVE ACTION TO DEVELOP A HUB FOR COMMUNITY HEALTH

Duquesne University's Center for Community-Engaged Teaching and Research (CETR) serves as the university's front door to connecting students and faculty members with community priorities and partners. In 2016 the CETR secured funding for a strategic planning process that would enable the university to expand and deepen its work with economically underserved neighborhoods surrounding the university's campus in downtown Pittsburgh, Pennsylvania. Nancy was brought in as a consultant to facilitate the strategic planning process.

In consultation with Nancy, members of a 25-person strategic planning committee were organized into three groups, each of which considered how members could use their assets to address a grand challenge that would energize a robust, national model partnership between Duquesne University and its adjacent neighborhoods. One group (the "Red Team"), composed of people with connections to health-related assets, decided to create a Center for Community Health and Well-Being that would bring together many disparate health assets and interests.

Red Team members decided that their first project in moving toward the goal of establishing the CETR was to identify current financial resources and gauge the level of interest and commitment from key stakeholders in the community and university. Before they left the meeting, they developed a 30-day action plan. One team member offered to coordinate a meeting with key community members, another member convened a meeting with key university members, another committed to investigate potential funding, and other team members indicated that they would assess the suitability of repurposing various community spaces for housing the Center's proposed range of activities.

The team continued to work together, at each meeting identifying their next critical action items and making sure that there was a clear plan for completion. After several months, the Red Team (along with the two other teams that had been launched) were ready to present their work – and a request for support – to the university's leadership.

As is often the case with collaborative initiatives, this one took place in a context of considerable change. By the time of the presentation, there had been some major transitions in the landscape: there was a new president at Duquesne, and turnover was underway at the CETR as well. While the presentation was well-received, the time was not right to move forward on new initiatives, and so far the idea has not moved forward.

However, the process of working together effectively – even if the original goal is still unrealized – opened up new opportunities. Primary among them was a new partnership between Duquesne's pharmacy school and the county health department. When the health department's pharmacist resigned, the leaders realized there was an alternative to their traditional approach to staffing: they decided to subcontract with the university to provide coverage for pharmacy services. This new partnership is laying the ground for future collaboration ahead.

Chapter 10

SET 30/30 MEETINGS TO REVIEW, LEARN, AND ADJUST (SKILL 9)

If you've ever moved into a new house or apartment, the first few months are full of learning things about your new home. Maybe there are strange creaks in the middle of the night, or perhaps the water pipes shake if the shower tap isn't at full strength. With the change of seasons comes another set of new discoveries: If you set the thermostat at 68 degrees, will it actually be 68 degrees in your living room? The piece of equipment that does this job – or not, as you may discover – is the thermostat. It measures the temperature in the room and then sends a signal to the heating system to adjust if needed until the temperature matches the level you set.

To make sure that agile strategy efforts stay on track, we use a feedback loop. This idea comes from industrial control systems, in which the loop helps maintain the stability of the system. The thermostat provides the feedback on the heating system, for example. A system without a feedback loop can spin out of control.

LEARNING LOOPS

A room thermostat monitors temperature more or less continuously. It's not taking any other information into account; for example, when spring comes around, we need the heating system less frequently, but the thermostat doesn't know it's spring – if it did, perhaps it would have already told the heating system to start its adjustment. Instead, the thermostat just keeps checking the room temperature and sends the data on. Each monitoring cycle is completely self-contained, unconnected from the previous ones.

Agile leaders need a specific kind of feedback loop: a *learning loop*. Unlike a thermostat, we don't want to start over every time – we want a feedback loop to provide information that can permanently upgrade our ability to do complex work together. Some of the best thinking about learning loops comes from management thinker Chris Argyris. He advocated for "double-loop learning"and gave this example:

> A thermostat that automatically turns on the heat whenever the temperature in a room drops below 68°F is a good example of single-loop learning. A thermostat that could ask, "Why am I set to 68°F?" and then explore whether some other temperature

might more economically achieve the goal of heating the room would be engaged in double-loop learning."

In other words, you want to build into your process regular "pauses" in which you can ask whether you are where you had planned to be, but also whether you have learned anything that tells you that those plans weren't the right ones in the first place. (Argyris, 2002)

Agile leaders need learning loops for two reasons. First, in complex systems we do not know what will work to change the performance of the system. We'll have to experiment to identify leverage points. Second, we need learning loops because circumstances change. The environment is not stable, so we will want to make adjustments along the way. When your team meets frequently to examine the results of your work and discuss adjustments to the next cycle, you are making sure that you have a learning loop.

We use the phrase 30/30 to refer to these meetings. The name comes from Ed's earliest work in Oklahoma City. As he was working with a team to develop a strategy for transforming the city's economy, his team met every 30 days to review their progress. The agenda was simple. What did we learn the last 30 days? And what will we do the next 30 days? In a 30/30, you check in on progress, review results, discuss needed changes and make adjustments. A 30/30 is simply shorthand for the next time your team will meet and what the agenda will be, in very broad terms. A 30/30 looks backward – at the last 30 days – and forward to the next 30 days.

The designation of 30/30 is flexible and may need to be adjusted as you go. When the environment is extremely turbulent, you may need to make these adjustments more often. Your network might use 7/7s, 14/14s, all the way to (very rarely) 180/180s. Our experience is that 30/30s are a good place to start.

BUILDING NEW HABITS

Learning loops are often compared to setting a new habit. Perhaps you already have habits that you have built into your life. Maybe you exercise three times a week, meditate 10 minutes each morning, read

30 minutes every day, or do some other regularly scheduled activity. It wouldn't do much good if you exercised just once a month – it's the fact that you've made it a habit that really provides the benefit to you. Setting a 30/30 is similar to this in many ways – its real power isn't in the meeting itself, it's in creating a new habit for working together.

Between the five authors of this book, we have more than 50 years of experience helping hundreds of groups adopt an agile strategy approach. When we review the initiatives we've had a part in, this is the skill that, more than any other, differentiates the successful groups from those that had more limited impact. Simply put, 30/30s provide the learning and accountability a team needs to make optimal choices and to stay engaged.

However, 30/30s do not need to be long. The more regularly you meet, the less time is needed at each meeting because team members know what the agenda is: they are ready to report in with results and to volunteer for the next steps. The level at which the team is learning becomes very high. The blame game disappears. Members find themselves enjoying accomplishing complex work and are eager to keep up the forward momentum.

The level of trust is also higher in teams that meet regularly over longer periods of time. Every time you meet, you are making a new set of micro-commitments to one another. That trust acts as fuel to help your team reach success.

With today's technology tools and platforms, there are many variations of how to meet and how to make each team member feel a part of something bigger than themselves. Ideally 30/30s are in person, as the transparency of an in-person meeting far exceeds a phone call. Second best is to use a videoconferencing medium and, if that is simply not possible, you can schedule a conference call. It's particularly important that the team meet in person for the first few check-ins. Our experience is that three to four in-person meetings seems to be the "magic number" for establishing trust and reliability – after those in-person meetings, videoconference or phone calls can be effective. No matter what the medium, it is critical to assure success that team members keep to the agreed-to meeting schedule.

PUTTING THE SKILL TO WORK: THE AGILE LEADER AS CONVENER

There are many opportunities to apply the 30/30 concept to committees, meetings, and projects you're a part of. Almost everyone appreciates meetings that are productive and efficiently managed. The agenda for a 30/30 meeting should be very clear and simple, and the meeting doesn't need to be long (30 to 60 minutes). You could use the following questions:

- What did we learn the last 30 days?
- Here's the outcome we've agreed to. Do we want to make any changes? Does everyone all still agree with the outcome we've chosen?
- Are we on track for what we're currently working on? How should we update our action plan?
- When and where will we next get together? Are there any communication problems we need to resolve?

The last question is in some ways the most important. Schedule your *next* meeting every time you meet. Don't leave this item until later – take care of it while everyone is together (some groups make this the first item on the agenda at each 30/30). Even if one or two people can't make the meeting, move forward. It is critical to establish the habit of convening regularly.

30/30 meetings help build a shared accountability and heightens the trust level between team members. Over time, you may find that you have a team member who consistently misses meetings or fails to complete an action, threatening the success of the group. It is important for this to be discussed at the meeting, with the focus on how we can engage the member more fully or (if needed) part ways with the member, so that others' work is not diminished by the person's lack of effort. Having 30/30 meetings helps you see these patterns quickly and helps you address them so the project does not suffer.

You can also use the 30/30 concept in your own life as you strive to be a better person and professional. Here are a few examples:

- You can commit to expanding your network through tools like LinkedIn where you can reconnect with people you know and regularly invite them to join a project you're working on.

- You can identify two people each month who need to meet each other, and make that happen through an introductory email.
- You can begin a new habit of watching a video every week that grows your knowledge.

Every 30 days, take a step back and ask yourself what you're learning and how it's having an impact. If you need to, adjust your habit to make it more effective.

Agile leaders convene regular but brief meetings that help sustain the momentum of a group's work. As 30/30s become a habit, teams build resilience and a knack for flexibility over time as they incorporate change into their projects and respond to new members, new assets and new networks. This strength-building will be key as the group begins to take on bigger projects.

CASE STUDY: HELPING A MUSIC CAPITAL PEN ITS NEXT HITS

If you're a music fan, you might have heard of the Muscle Shoals area of Alabama, on the Tennessee River. Many of the best-known musical groups of the past 50 years have recorded at one of the studios in the region. But beyond the music scene, this mostly rural region has struggled. In 2014, the aftermath of the Great Recession was still very much being felt: that year the region lost another 1,900 manufacturing jobs to factory closures. University of North Alabama (UNA) students were asking why the region did not have appropriate jobs for their skills upon graduation, forcing them to seek opportunities elsewhere. At the Shoals Chamber of Commerce (SCC), young business leaders, including several UNA alumni, challenged the organization to justify why they should keep their newly established ventures in the Shoals. Responding to these dual demands required a cohesive and robust economic development effort to drive the region's growth.

UNA, the SCC, and the Shoals Business Incubator established a new collaboration that would change the region's economic trajectory. Named the Shoals Shift Project, this unique collaborative effort focuses on leveraging existing assets and developing creative ways to grow a digital economy in the region. The group focuses on strategies to retain UNA graduates by promoting the development of new ventures as well as generating new twenty-first-century jobs in existing industries.

The collaborative team is deeply committed to this work. They have consciously embraced an approach of "doing, not waiting," and have met every four to six weeks since the project launched in 2014. This rhythm has allowed the partners to experiment and try new ideas. For example, they launched a business plan competition in 2014; rather than taking a year to plan, they moved forward and announced the competition immediately, eager to learn if there was sufficient community support for such a venture. There was – tapping their own networks, they raised the necessary $15,000 and hosted a successful competition.

The community has rallied around the collaboration and progress has been swift. Shoals Shift hosts a suite of events with more than 250 competitors that are now part of the region's business calendar and culture. The team raises more than $200,000 annually, and in 2016, their efforts were rewarded with almost $1 million from the Appalachian Regional Commission. The initiative was also one of three finalists for the 2018 Phi Kappa Phi Excellence in Innovation award, along with two better-known universities. More than 200 UNA students have been trained in entrepreneurial approaches and the project has birthed 15 UNA student start-ups that are raising capital and creating jobs – all to create a brighter future for the region's residents.

Chapter 11

NUDGE, CONNECT, AND PROMOTE TO REINFORCE NEW HABITS (SKILL 10)

If you've ever tried to establish a new habit, you know that it can be a considerable challenge. It might be losing weight, kicking a smoking habit, starting an exercise routine, cleaning up clutter in your house, or changing your morning routine so your kids get to school without everyone tearing their hair out.

You start with optimism and a burst of energy – it seems so simple! But gyms are full in January and empty by March for a reason – it is hard to make a habit "stick." There's no lack of suggestions that might help – do it for at least 21 days, pair up with someone for support, do things in small increments rather than thinking change has to happen all at once, modify your environment so you're not triggered in the same way . . . and on and on. You might need to do one or all of these things to be successful.

We said in Chapter 1 that "doing differently" when it comes to collaborative networks needed to become a way of life, a set of new habits. These habits – the ways in which you use the skills we've described in this book – are no different than the resolutions we make in January. They seem simple, and in fact they are. But, *simple is not the same thing as easy.* You need to find ways to make the habits stick to be successful over the long term. There are three specific kinds of activities that will make these new habits of collaboration more likely to be permanent. These activities are *also* habits – it's like getting into the habit of setting your alarm clock earlier, so that you can get into the habit of making it to the gym in the morning.

Before getting specific about what's involved in this skill, we need to return to the idea of shared leadership. While there is no top or bottom to a network, effective networks do have strong cores, agile leaders who provide guidance. Agile leaders take the initiative to be responsible for the health of the network itself. One person can take the lead, and the role can rotate over time, but to return to a theme we've discussed earlier: if it's vaguely assumed that the network will thrive on its own, it won't. Agile leaders help the new network that is established in a collaboration to become more resilient and to grow over time.

NUDGING

The first way agile leaders maintain the momentum of a network is to *nudge everyone to move ideas into action and complete their tasks*. In nudging, we are acknowledging the reality that most people will not do what needs to be done all of the time without this kind of reinforcement. We *all* need an extra push (at least some of the time) to get us to do our part in the new collaborative venture.

When we nudge, we are really doing two things: most obviously, we are ensuring that a particular task is completed. Less obvious but more important is the second function of nudging: we are establishing positive norms for the group. A norm can be thought of as an unwritten rule of behavior that is unnatural. For example, we learn in school that we raise our hand to speak. We aren't born knowing that we need to do that – but very quickly, it becomes second nature and we can't imagine behaving in any other way. It is "normal."

How can we nudge in such a way that a project moves forward, and beyond that so that the group becomes more effective? There are two approaches:

First, there is proactive nudging. By proactive, we mean that you explicitly urge each person to complete their assignment. You check in with others in the group by phone or in person, or – increasingly – use email or texting to encourage people to fulfill their commitments.

You'll want to think carefully about the people you are trying to nudge and what approach might work for each of them – what is effective for one person may not work for another. Those of us who are parents of more than one child have learned this the hard way: a particular kind of nudge to one child may result in the desired behavior, but may make another dig their heels in and refuse to budge. You'll have to observe and adjust as you learn what works.

Since much of our communication is now through email or text, it's worth considering how we might effectively "digitally nudge." There is some interesting research behind this idea. In *Inside the Nudge Unit*, author David Halpern discusses how the right kind of digital nudges can increase the chances of influencing someone's behavior. For instance, in programs to encourage job seekers to attend job fairs, sending a standard, generic text message resulted in about 1 in 10 people turning up. Adding the recipient's name at the beginning of the text increased the proportion turning up at a fair by five percentage points to 15%. If the advisor also added their own name? The number turning up rose even further, to 18%. And if the advisor instead wrote: "I've booked you a place . . . Good luck!" the proportion turning up rose to an impressive 27%, a nearly threefold increase from the original response. UCLA Researcher Shlomo Ben-Artzi suggests that pointing to and celebrating the behavior of others who are exhibiting the actions or habits you want others to emulate can influence behaviors even more. For instance, if an entire neighborhood is being challenged to beautify their yards, sending a photo or video of one of the spruced-up yards with a message like "Check out the Crespos' beautiful yard!" can make the nudge even stronger.

There's also more subtle nudging. This moves us into the realm of *behavioral economics*, a field for which Richard Thaler won the Nobel Prize for economics in 2017; beyond his theoretical contributions to the field, Thaler has written a number of books to help noneconomists understand the important underlying principles. The key concept behind behavioral economics is that environments encourage particular choices. Finding a way to change the environment so that the desired behavior "just happens" can be much easier than having to work in a proactive fashion. The classic example (which Thaler had an indirect hand in) is the challenge of getting Vanguard employees to save for their retirement. The traditional approach is to provide new employees with information about 401(k) plans, and a way to sign up to participate. This method usually results in about 40% of the employees taking part. However, a new 2006 law gave employers another option: rather than providing employees with a form to sign up, they could require that employees opt *out* if they didn't want to participate by sign a form to that effect. The change seems subtle – a few words on the materials for new employees – until you consider the results. More than 90% of the employees in the Vanguard study chose to participate.

Until now, we've focused primarily on nudging as a mechanism to get individuals to act. But let's step back and think about the group as a whole. Beyond the specifics of whether a particular task is accomplished, what you are aiming for is building an environment in which the group members know they can trust one another. As we said in Chapter 2, trust is built when we align our words with our actions. The micro-commitments people make to one another are the words – the nudge helps ensure that the circle is closed. As these fulfilled micro-commitments accumulate, the group trust increases. It's as if you are constructing a rope. If you look carefully at a rope, you'll see that the strands are twisted together. This has a practical function in terms of being able to handle the rope more easily. But beyond that, the twist ensures that tension is distributed evenly along the rope, and no individual strand is supporting too much of the load. This is important because the stronger the rope, the heavier the object it can pull. A group with a high level of trust has the capacity – the resiliency – to take on big challenges.

There is another kind of trust being built as well – it is the trust that the group has in *you* to keep them on track. You may feel as if you are being intrusive, or "bugging" people, and sometimes a person's reaction ("would you just leave me alone?") may reinforce this fear. Look at your role differently: what the members of your group are most afraid of is that they are wasting their time. All of us have been members of groups that failed to fulfill their purpose not because the approach was wrong, but because the effort was incomplete. Things just fell apart. If you were one of the people who did step up, but others did not, you may have felt that others took advantage of your goodwill and integrity. With nudging, you are doing something different. You are keeping the momentum going. You are keeping people aligned and energized. There may still be someone who doesn't do what they said they will do, but the other people in the group will feel protected – there is someone looking out for them.

CONNECTING

Another habit of agile leaders that strengthens a network is to *connect* new people and other networks to it. While increased trust binds the strands of a rope together, you can also increase the ability of the rope to lift a heavy object by adding more strands. In connecting, you intentionally seek to grow the network. As we saw when we discussed the structure of a network in Chapter 1, networks have porous boundaries.

Connecting is taking an active role in helping people move across that boundary to be more tightly connected to your network.

Each addition to the network brings new resources and assets that might be instrumental in the group's future work. In some cases you'll be aware of a particular need – for a physical asset like a meeting space, for example. Other times you're not exactly sure what someone can contribute but it seems like they should be connected to your network so that if the right moment arises, there's already the start of a relationship. Ed is especially expert at forging connections like this by "closing the triangle" (he learned this clever and simple way to build networks from his colleague Valdis Krebs, a gifted consultant in the field of social networks; Valdis was the creator of the iPhone network "map" we shared in Chapter 1). Ed identifies someone inside his network who has a common interest with a person he's just met, and sends an email like the following:

> Terri, meet Joe. I'm introducing you to one another because I think you might have some common interests and could benefit from meeting.
>
> Terri is part of our group on regional competitiveness. She's one of the vice presidents at the Chamber of Commerce and has a lot of experience working with overseas companies considering a presence in the metro area.
>
> I met Joe last week at a conference. Joe has just moved here with Acme Inc., which is starting to consider growing its activity in Latin America and is interested in learning more about the business culture there.
>
> I think the two of you would have an interesting conversation about your mutual interests and experience. I'll leave it to you to connect further.

We talked about group size in Chapter 2, and the prospect of growing your network may mean that at some point you start to bump up against the upper limit for a high-functioning group. When this happens, you will probably need to divide into two groups to pursue different projects. Other members of the network will need to step up as agile leaders as well, and they may need your assistance in doing so.

In training others to become more effective collaborators, the metaphor of teaching a child to ride a bike may be helpful. First, the child needs to see someone else successfully riding – maybe they are in the child seat attached to the back of your bike. Then, they give it a try; there may be training wheels at first, but soon the wheels are off and you're hanging on to the seat running alongside. Finally, you don't need to hang on any more, and while they may be a bit shaky at first (and angry that you let go!), they're quickly zipping around the neighborhood.

In the same way, help others build their skills by first explaining what you're doing as you're doing it, then having them practice with you nearby, and then letting them lead on their own. Just as they were for you, these new ways of working together may feel a bit frightening at first, but new leaders will gain confidence with experience.

While we're talking about connecting, it's also worth mentioning "disconnecting." The porous boundaries go both ways – sometimes a person who's been close to the hub of your network someone with whom you've worked closely, needs to step away. Perhaps their job responsibilities have changed, they're moving to a different part of the country, or they've welcomed a child into their family. Or, perhaps they've realized that they don't really *want* to be part of a group in which they're expected to participate actively (or as a person in one of our workshops said recently, "I didn't realize you wanted me to actually *do* something!"). Saying good-bye is also part of nurturing networks.

PROMOTING

The third habit to cultivate is that of *promoting*. Unless your group is engaged in classified espionage, you want to publicize your successes. This helps attract more people to your network that you might not have had access to otherwise. Promotion is particularly important if yours is the kind of group that doesn't have much in the way of access to financial resources. People with money make decisions about where to invest it based in part on their calculation of risk – and the best predictor of low risk is a track record of achievement. Even if your successes are small, they communicate that you're a good investment prospect.

How you promote your work can vary wildly. It could be everything from an intentional but informal conversation with a decision maker in the company cafeteria to an all-out social media blitz. We can't tell you what makes sense for your group, and there are plenty of books out there on promotion, marketing, and social media that are better resources. However, everyone in your group should be prepared to explain what you're doing in what's sometimes called an "elevator pitch" – a clear description in less than two minutes (the average time for a ride in an elevator).

Nudging, connecting, and promoting are all ways agile leaders ensure that efforts don't wither on the vine. They are habits to build, and like every new habit, they take time and consistent attention, and some may come easier than others. They are the skills that turn a group's good idea into real impact for a company, community, or organization.

PUTTING THE SKILL TO WORK: THE AGILE LEADER AS CHIEF DOING OFFICER

In our work, we often call the person who takes on nudging, connecting, and promoting the "Chief Doing Officer"or CDO. If we had to sum up the CDO's job in one phrase, it would be "helping a group grow into new habits."

There isn't a specific experience or title or degree that is a prerequisite for being a CDO—we've seen people from all walks of life do it very successfully—but their one personal trait that is critical is emotional intelligence. Emotional intelligence is the ability to be aware of one's own and others' emotions, and to use that information to choose the correct behaviors in a particular situation. In our context, it is important because a such a large part of the CDO role is persuading others.

Like other kinds of intelligence, emotional intelligence is largely something that people have as a result of their genetics, temperament, and/or early upbringing – you can't really change it to any large degree, although knowing your limitations *will* help you know when to ask for help. Unfortunately, the people with the lowest levels of emotional intelligence are also the least self-aware about it. One "red flag" is that you find people frequently offended by something you say or do, yet you think they're overreacting. If this is the case, or if you're just not sure about your own emotional intelligence, you might need to ask a trusted peer for some honest feedback. If your emotional intelligence is low, you may need to ask someone else in your group to take on at least some of the functions we describe in this chapter.

First things first: it's important to let a group know in advance you'll be nudging. Make sure people understand that your nudging isn't a criticism of anyone, but rather a way to help the group achieve what they all want.

Considering the concepts of behavioral economics may lead you to some creative nudging approaches. How could you establish environmental cues that help people behave in the ways you need them to – or, as Richard Thaler terms it, how could you be mindful of the "choice architecture?" A few approaches that we have seen include:

- Setting up a shared folder in which each person deposits some sort of "report" on what they've done;
- Using a shared document as a checklist. Use it in a positive fashion – perhaps there's a line for each person to complete about the results of their work. Do not make it punitive, such as a list of people who have not done their part;
- Using "reply all" (carefully) to spread the word when someone has completed their work or discovered something interesting;
- Organizing a "field trip" to see a successful region, organization, or team in action. You don't need to spell out the lessons; just exposure to what is effective speaks loudly and helps groups set higher expectations for themselves.

Cultivate the habit of inviting new people into your work. Each one will bring their assets with them and these may open up new opportunities. Tell people about what you're doing and invite them in. Everyone is busy, but there is almost nothing more attractive than a group that is *getting things done*. Ask your fellow group members to do the same kind of connecting – regularly ask one another, "Is there anyone else that we think might want to join us, who would bring new resources that we need?" Look especially to the boundary spanners in your group – those people who are in multiple networks. Boundary spanners usually are spanners precisely because they enjoy making connections between people. They're matchmakers (professionally speaking) by temperament.

When you or another group member issues an invitation, make sure the person understands that they're going to be expected to be full participants – it's not an advisory committee that exists only on paper. They'll be making micro-commitments along with everyone else.

Agile leaders understand that their leadership doesn't end when a meeting is over. They build relationships with people within the group so that they can encourage them to live up to the micro-commitments they've made. They also nurture relationships with people that aren't in the group – spreading the word about the good work underway and looking for ways to connect them to the network in some way. They are both active participants in and cheerleaders for the groups they lead.

CASE STUDY: TURNING MICRO-COMMITMENTS INTO LARGER INNOVATIONS

We introduced a large defense contractor's quest for a condition-based maintenance solution in the introduction to this book. As we examine this final skill of agile leadership, we want to illustrate what this skill looks like "on the ground" by giving you a peek at the process that was involved in developing and implementing that initiative. The company, a global aerospace and security firm, has put a high priority on innovation. In 2015, the company's leadership at the Moorestown, New Jersey facility talked with New Jersey Innovation Institute's (NJII) Tim Franklin about possibilities for engaging NJII in a partnership to conduct what amounted to a set of innovation experiments. The thinking behind these experiments was to introduce the firm to new innovation tools that could aid the company in accessing nontraditional sources of innovation in service of a better, faster, cheaper path from idea to deployable solution. One of these experiments centered on employing an open innovation methodology to generate product solutions addressing the ability to better predict when equipment failures would occur ("condition-based maintenance" or CBM) in advanced defense systems.

Tim invited Ed and Scott to help guide the process, and designated Mike van Ter Sluis, NJII's executive director of Innovation Services, as the "Chief Doing Officer" for the project. NJII put out a call for New Jersey companies with expertise in various competencies associated with CBM (e.g., sensors, data analytics, visualization, augmented reality), inviting them to be part of co-developing a CBM solution with the defense contractor. Mike, Ed, and Scott designed and conducted a series of workshops to consider how they might collaborate in solution development. The objectives were to understand how CBM had been applied in other industries, how current technologies represented by the companies at the workshop could be combined to create a solution, and to draft an investment prospectus for the defense contractor to share with the Department of Defense. About ninety companies from throughout the state responded to the invitation to participate.

Mike carefully tracked the micro-commitments of various participants in the process, nudging them as needed to ensure the project work continued on track. He carefully documented project discussions and action items, ensuring that all team members had visibility to all parts of the discussions and developments. Mike communicated regularly with with the client to engage additional subject matter experts as the project developed (connecting new people to the network), and he took primary responsibility for creating the prospectus that pulled together the group's work. Once the prospectus was completed, Mike organized a meeting for the group to present its roadmap and proof of concept to leadership at the defense contractor (promoting the group's work as a potential solution).

Consistent follow-up was the key to turning the good ideas that the ninety companies generated at the original workshops into the practical and realistic plans that were needed. "'Nudging' seems different for corporate clients (at least for open innovation tech development)," says Mike, "because there is a very clear goal in mind. So, I might describe it better as 'driving' toward a client expectation, which feels more intense than nudging. It was a significant effort. I was responsible for collating all the assets in a coherent project proposal/investment perspective. At the end of the day, it was NJII that was responsible for a deliverable – even though we are leveraging the assets of a network that we at NJII did not own or control.

"In this project, it was a very selective, narrowing effort. That is quite different than when I've used this skill in regional economic development. There, I've been trying to grow the network exponentially by bringing new people and assets in. But the idea of close attention to follow-up is critical in both kinds of work."

Chapter 12

TEN SKILLS. GOT IT. NOW WHAT?

I n the past ten chapters, we introduced you to ten different skills. You can use any of these skills with the groups, teams, and organizations you're a part of and that are facing complex challenges. They take practice to master, but you will immediately see productivity gains. Fewer wasted hours in meetings. Less confusion over direction. More excitement and engagement in the work that you do.

Each of these skills stands on its own. Give some forethought, for example, to the strategic conversations you need to have. Take some time to make sure these conversations take place in both a safe place and safe space. This alone can be transformational; we've seen how that first skill, applied and reinforced, begins to change a tide of bad conversational habits. When people feel safe, they are more open to revealing and sharing their assets.

The second skill holds equal potential. Over and over, we've heard from groups that just talking about what the question *should* be – not even trying to answer it yet – has completely changed the conversations they are having. They've gone from having to beg people to attend meetings to having to train more leaders, because so many people want to be part of a group that is daring to dream a new dream.

Here's another example. If you're faced with several opportunities but have only enough time or money resources to do one, pull out the Big Easy matrix. You'll find that the two dimensions of this matrix help you find a good balance point between impact and ease of implementation. In 1772, Benjamin Franklin, writing to his friend, the eminent British scientist Joseph Priestly, explained how he made difficult decisions between two choices. He divided a piece of paper by drawing a line down the middle. On one side he listed "pro" reasons. On the other side he listed "con" reasons. He also attached weights to different reasons. He then compared his pro list to his con list to reach a decision. You can think of the Big Easy as a continuation of this tradition: using commonsense tools to make complex decisions. The Big Easy is a simple way to make your strategic intuition explicit and visible, either individually or in a group.

At this point we want to pause for a moment. As we near the end of this book, we might owe you a bit of an apology. We say "might" because whether an apology is needed depends on the expectations you had when you picked up this book. We thought long and hard about the title and the perspective from which we wrote the book. We eventually settled on the perspective of "leadership." But we do not mean leadership in the traditional sense of the inspired individual sitting on top of the organization.

If you picked up this book thinking you would get insight on ten skills *you* can master to be *the* agile leader for your company, team, committee, or organization, then we do apologize. Why? Because you won't be able to completely master all ten. There will likely be one or two for which you are already very well-suited; these are in your DNA or you've mastered them through years of experience. Several of the others you'll probably be able to develop to some level of expertise. At least a few, however, will probably always feel like writing with your nondominant hand – legible, but not effortless. Among the five of us who wrote this book, we each have different strengths: for example, Janyce is a master at developing appreciative questions. Ed's great at drawing undiscovered assets out of people.

If the title of the book were "Ten Skills for *the* Agile Leader," we really would owe you an apology and maybe even your money back. Fortunately, we didn't use that phrasing. Instead, we promised ten skills for agile *leadership* and the leadership we have in mind rests with the collective, not the individual. Our focus is not on the individual leader but, rather, on leadership as a *shared characteristic of a group or a team*. Elsewhere in the book, we've used the phrase "distributed leadership" or "shared leadership."

Shared leadership is defined as leadership that is carried out by the team as a whole rather than solely by a single designated individual. As we pointed out in Chapter 9, there is a growing body of research that points to shared leadership in teams and organizations as being positively associated with team effectiveness and productivity; and, that the relationship between shared leadership and effectiveness is *even stronger* when the team's work is highly complex. For some of us, that is a counterintuitive notion, because complexity can feel like chaos and in the midst of chaos we feel better when someone stands up and shouts, "I'm in charge."

To better understand why shared leadership is effective in accomplishing complex work we go to the work of psychologist W. Ross Ashby. He wrote extensively about something called the *Law of*

Requisite Variety. It is an idea so closely associated with him that it is sometimes referred to as "Ashby's Law." Ashby pointed out that a complex environment is one that has a lot of variety, or a lot of variables. That's what makes it complex. Ashby said that any attempt to deal that complexity must have an *equal*, or requisite, amount of variety. Ashby's law has been stated and validated as a law of cybernetics (the science of communications and control systems). But if we dig a little deeper, Ashby's insight opens the door to an interesting and important understanding of why diversity matters when we work with complex systems and messy challenges. It's why shared leadership has become so important. Most of the time, a single leader will simply not have enough variety of experiences, skills, and expertise to manage their way through a complex situation.

In his book *The Difference*, Scott Page guides us further down this path of considering how our diverse qualities as individuals contribute to a group's functioning. By diversity, Page is not thinking about our identity – the external manifestations of diversity that we see in racial, ethnic, or gender differences. He refers instead to *cognitive diversity*, the different ways in which each of us sees the world. It's our internal differences, our cognitive skills, that matter. These other categories of diversity matter as well, but a group that looks diverse on the outside could still be thinking quite similarly on the inside.

Think about this point for a moment. With the complex challenges we face, we are dealing with large networks that we cannot see from a single viewpoint. Think of climate change, or a company trying to accelerate innovation, or gun violence in a poor neighborhood. While we can see certain manifestations of these challenges, we cannot see the underlying human systems that produce what we perceive. Our economy, our communities, our organizations: they all consist of shifting human networks embedded in other networks. Page is pointing out that we need a diverse set of cognitive skills, if we are to have any hope of understanding, designing, and guiding these networks.

It's one thing to accept that we need this kind of diversity, but quite another to figure out how to use the concept to make teams more effective. At the Purdue Agile Strategy Lab we are using a powerful team diagnostic tool developed by our partner Human Insight in The Netherlands. With this tool (called the AEM-Cube®), we are learning how to assemble cognitively and strategically diverse teams. We are understanding why some people are really good at Skills 3, 4, and 5 and not so good at Skills 8, 9, and 10 (or vice versa). By engaging the full spectrum of our diversity, we can find the path toward more resilient, sustainable, and prosperous organizations and communities.

If you've paid attention to the stories we've told throughout this book, you'll notice that these were not primarily stories of individuals but of groups of people. In writing the book, we went back and visited with the people that were involved in each of those stories – even though one or more of us had been involved in the work at the time, we wanted to hear what had happened since as well as their reflections after some time had passed. When we asked them about their efforts, they didn't tell us stories of individual "champions" or stand-out individuals; they told stories of shared leadership. Even when they're queried about their work and someone directly asks something like, "Who's the leader of this effort?" the answer usually includes several people, or even "We all are."

Looking back, we have described ten skills that you can use to build and strengthen collaborative efforts. You can practice and share each of them:

1. Building a safe space for deep and focused conversations.
2. Using an appreciative question to frame your conversation.
3. Identifying the assets at your disposal, including the hidden ones.
4. Linking and leveraging your assets to create new opportunities.
5. Identifying a big opportunity where you can generate momentum.
6. Rewriting your opportunity as a strategic outcome with measurable characteristics.
7. Defining a small starting project to start moving toward your outcome.
8. Creating a short-term action plan in which everyone takes a small step.
9. Meeting every 30 days to review progress, adjust, and plan for the next 30 days.

10. Nudging, connecting, and promoting to reinforce your new habits of collaboration.

PUTTING IT ALL TOGETHER: STRATEGIC DOING

While each of the individual skills is a powerful tool, these skills also work together within an elegantly coherent framework. We have learned how to build complex collaborations following the simple ideas we have shared. To understand this point, think of a flock of geese or starlings. Their complex, unfolding formations emerge from each bird following a small set of simple rules. The same is true for human collaborations. Complex collaborations emerge when we follow a small set of simple rules. These rules – really, just the implementation of each of the skills –embed a lot of practices that academics have found valuable in a wide range of academic fields including psychology, strategic management, organizational development, cognitive science, behavioral economics, complexity economics, and cultural anthropology.

We've spent more than 25 years developing this coherent framework, and 10 or so learning how to teach it to others. We have tested it with space scientists at NASA and community leaders in Flint; faculty from many disciplines at more than sixty universities; engineers at a large defense contractor and small technology companies; executives and university administrators. We've worked with workforce, economic, and community development professionals; CEOs and management teams; educators and students; researchers and administrators; and government employees and elected officials.

In most situations, we introduce this framework by presenting the challenge as of one of designing collaborative conversations. We tend to think that conversations "just happen," but when we're facing complex challenges we can't leave it to chance – the conversation needs to be intentionally designed. Collaborative conversations start with what we call the Four Questions, shown in Figure 12.1:

1. What could we do? What are all the possible opportunities before us – using only the assets that we already have – that might address our concerns?

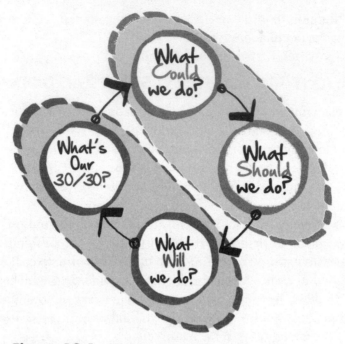

Figure 12.1   The Four Questions of Strategic Doing.

2. What should we do? We can't do everything; which, out of all the opportunities, should we pursue, and what would success look like?
3. What will we do? Where will we start and what are the commitments we are making to each other to begin that project?
4. What's our 30/30? When, exactly, are we going to get back together to share what we've done, so that we can learn from our experience, adjust if we need to, and plot out our next set of commitments?

You can probably see how each of the skills fits somewhere in this sequence. Skills 1 and 2 help you set the stage for productive, collaborative conversations. Skills 3 and 4 are the components of "What Could We Do?" – identifying new opportunities that draw on the assets we already have. Skills 5 and 6 make up "What Should We Do?" – picking the right opportunity and exploring it to make sure we are sharing what success looks like to all of us. Skills 7 and 8 become "What Will We

Do?" – defining a small project we can do together in a short time frame to test out our idea. And "What's our 30/30?" draws on Skills 9 and 10, in which we make sure to come back together regularly and keep moving forward. As we do, we draw in new people and assets as we go.

As we work through these questions, we may come to a decision point for some reason: we finish our starting project. One of our ideas turns out to be impossible. Someone makes a pool of money available. What now? We start again with the first question, "What Could We Do?" It's a circle, after all.

We started this book by telling you that the set of skills in this book make up Strategic Doing. This is true, but it's when we use the skills in this *particular* way, asking the Four Questions in an iterative fashion, that Strategic Doing can be the most transformative. It's fundamentally different from traditional strategic planning, which is often a long, drawn-out process for making investment decisions. Yet, we learned long ago that the more rigid and complex protocols of traditional strategic planning do not work well in a world increasingly driven by networks. We still face these difficult decisions about where to invest our limited time and resources, but we need to make the decisions in a very different fashion.

When we decided that we needed an entirely new discipline of strategy, we had to start with a simple question: What do we mean by strategy? We decided to impose a rigorous definition. As we described in the first chapter, an effective strategy answers two questions: *Where we are going?* and *How we will get there?* If we can answer these two questions, we have an effective strategy. Using this rigorous definition, we can quickly see why so many strategic planning efforts fail. They do not adequately answer these questions in a way that inspires engagement.

We designed the four questions of Strategic Doing to guide groups in filling that gap. The first two questions of Strategic Doing – What could we do? and What should we do? – give us the destination. They answer "Where are we going?" The second two questions of Strategic Doing – What will we do? And What's our 30/30? — provide us with a pathway, answering "How will we get there?" In traditional strategic planning, these questions are revisited at long intervals – at best, every year; more often, every 5 or 10 years. In contrast, in

Strategic Doing we see that strategy *emerges* from a shared discipline of asking and answering these simple but not easy questions over and over. In this way, as we accumulate learning by doing, we refine our strategy. We build trust, and we design what's next. In the world of collaboration and networks, strategy becomes more like software development. Continuous iteration and improvement moves us forward to where we want to go.

Most of the case studies earlier in the book are of groups that used a comprehensive Strategic Doing approach – we've just focused in on one particular aspect of their story to illustrate the skill highlighted in that chapter. To explain more about how the approach works, let's turn our attention to some of the ways you can use Strategic Doing: as an individual, with a small group, or in a large initiative. We've also included a few more examples of our work which illustrate how a comprehensive Strategic Doing approach plays out.

USING STRATEGIC DOING AS AN INDIVIDUAL

The four questions of Strategic Doing provide you with a convenient template to design a collaborative conversation. One of our colleagues puts a map of the Strategic Doing cycle on the back of her office door. As she talks to colleagues on the phone, she refers to that list. "If we're not answering one of those questions," she says, "then this isn't a strategic conversation. We are not working on our collaboration." It helps her refocus her calls on doing meaningful work together rather than just having a "check-in."

Scott has another application, one that any parent of a teenager will appreciate. One day he asked his son an appreciative question: "What would it look like if your room was clean almost all of the time?" Caught off-guard by the question, his son replied, "Well, you wouldn't tell me I couldn't go somewhere because my room wasn't clean." (There's a measurable outcome!). Now Scott and his son can use that question to explore "What could we do?" It's not as if the room is suddenly always immaculate, but Strategic Doing has allowed him to have a different kind of conversation with his son, one that is hopefully much more productive.

Ed tells another story. Traveling to Stuttgart, Germany, Ed was exploring a collaboration with a German research institute, Fraunhofer IAO. He was able to arrange a two-hour meeting with two of the principals in a research team on innovation. Ed was interested in exploring potential collaborations between Purdue and Fraunhofer IAO in innovation. He didn't tell them he was using Strategic Doing, but in his own mind, Ed was using the Four Questions to organize the conversation. During the meeting, he divided the time and made sure to get through all four questions. He moved the conversation along by asking these questions. On the airplane home, he drafted a strategic action plan that identified twelve potential opportunities, focused on two opportunities to start, and set forth both a starting project and an action plan. This strategic action plan has served as the foundation for a partnership that continues to strengthen each year.

Peter Drucker, the famed management scholar, said, "The important and difficult job is never to find the right answers, it is to find the right question." Leadership in networks mostly involves guiding conversations by asking questions. Strategic Doing provides a powerful set of simple questions, so you can design and lead your own collaborative conversations.

USING STRATEGIC DOING IN A SMALL GROUP

If you're part of a task force, committee, or work team, you can use Strategic Doing to guide your work by using the skills sequentially. Think about a safe place, decide what the framing question is, and start your work together by talking about what assets you have. That's Skills 1–3. The rest follow in turn, with the caveat that Skill 10 is one that is ongoing, throughout the group's work.

A participant in one of our Strategic Doing workshops came to us afterward and asked, "Could I use this approach in my synagogue?" Indeed, several participants have used Strategic Doing with their churches and other faith communities. Facing a relatively large problem with relatively few resources is a common challenge for these groups. Designing conversations with Strategic Doing opens the door to more creative, horizontal thinking within the group.

Within the Purdue Agile Strategy Lab, Ed, Scott, and Liz use Strategic Doing to adjust the lab's strategy weekly. Instead of 30/30s we use 7/7s, because our environment is continuously shifting. We keep our central framing question in the back of our minds: "Imagine that the Purdue Agile Strategy Lab transformed the way strategy and collaboration are taught in universities across the globe. What would that look like?" We continuously look for the Big Easy opportunities that can help us answer that question. These opportunities are highly visible engagements that can serve as learning opportunities to everyone involved. We look for a local university partner, so we can replicate, scale, and sustain our work. When new opportunities pop up to fit our Big Easy criteria, we quickly make adjustments.

Here is a good example. Not long ago, we got a call from Yo-Yo Ma's office. A world-renowned cellist, Yo-Yo is deeply interested in moving arts and cultural education to the center of conversations in our communities. Yo-Yo had heard about our work in Strategic Doing, and he wanted to know if we could help design and guide a workshop for civic leaders in Youngstown, Ohio. The trick involved timing. Yo-Yo's performance in Ohio was only a week out. Could we move that fast? We jumped at the opportunity. In our 7/7 meeting, we quickly made adjustments to enable us to seize the opportunity while keeping our other priorities on track.

Here's another example: we use Strategic Doing *on* Strategic Doing. The development of this new discipline is guided by a core team of about ten people, drawn from all over the United States. Each has been using the discipline for at least several years, and as a group we are committed to seeing it grow. Three times a year, we meet someplace for 1.5 days. During these work sessions, we organize our agenda using the four questions. One of us serves as a guide to keep us on track and aligned. Indeed, this book represents a Big Easy opportunity that emerged from one of our strategy sessions. For years, people have been pressing Ed to write a book on Strategic Doing, and for years he has deflected. The reason: until we had enough people who could teach people the ten skills of Strategic Doing and support them in using them, what was the point of writing a book? We now have a sufficiently large group of universities engaged with us to offer Strategic Doing training at least once a month somewhere in the world.

Equally important, we have a large group of people with enough deep experience to both support the growth of Strategic Doing and to write a book.

USING STRATEGIC DOING WITH A LARGE INITIATIVE

In a larger context, Strategic Doing can be the new "operating system" for organizational or ecosystem transformation. It can (over time) help establish new, more productive patterns of thinking and behavior within an organization or community.

We gave you a window into a project Liz was part of in Chapter 8: an initiative to transform the undergraduate engineering experience at fifty universities. We focused on starting projects in that chapter, but the teams used Strategic Doing to manage their work more generally, starting with coming up with a framing question for their work.

As we discussed earlier, by the end of the three-year timeframe, these 50 teams had launched more than 500 collaborative projects. Their projects included new courses and certificates, new university policies to give students more incentives to create new products, new "makerspaces," even whole new university centers. In following up with the teams, Liz uncovered an even more important insight. The most productive teams consistently used (on average) eight of the ten skills of Strategic Doing. The least productive teams reported consistently using only two rules (again, on average). Although our research was not set up to examine causation (universities are complex places with many dynamics at work) we do see a strong correlation. We are continuing this line of research through our lab at Purdue. Our hypothesis is that following the Strategic Doing discipline makes teams and organizations more productive, and over time makes major transformations possible.

In another community, civic leaders in Rockford, Illinois, led by Rena Cotsones at Northern Illinois University (NIU), have used Strategic Doing to strengthen their aerospace companies. This critical sector of the Rockford economy is threatened by a looming shortage of engineering talent. In collaboration with industry partners and the local community college, NIU created a community-based, industry-integrated workforce development solution to address the demand for engineers. Rockford area students can now earn bachelor's degrees in mechanical engineering and applied manufacturing technology without traveling to NIU's main campus 40 miles away in DeKalb. Third and fourth year NIU courses are taught by NIU professors on the Rock Valley (Community) College (RVC) campus. Students have paid internships with area companies and are mentored by local NIU and RVC alumni.

In recognition of the importance of this initiative, local industry partners launched the "Engineering our Future" fundraising campaign and raised $6 million in nine months to support the program. The president of the lead donor company, Woodward, continues to host weekly Monday morning meetings with the higher education, industry, and community leadership team to ensure the successful operation and growth of the program. Using Strategic Doing, civic leaders in Rockford designed clear pathways from high school to community college to university to career. The initiative won a 2017 award of excellence by the University Economic Development Association.

Here's a final example. On the Space Coast in Florida in 2011, the future was clear – so clear, in fact, that it froze civic leaders. The space shuttle was shutting down, and the region's economy was facing a major transition. Lisa Rice, a workforce development professional, reached out to us with a simple question: "Can Strategic Doing help us?" For more than two years, civic leaders on the Space Coast had been trying to figure out a strategy for the dislocation that would take place when the space shuttle ceased operating. Despite multiple community meetings, they had not come up with any concrete actions. We did not have much time. Lisa's call came within a few months of the shutdown. We quickly organized an open forum. We organized tables around what we thought might be opportunities for the region.

When we opened the door, we saw a large group of people migrate toward one renewable energy table. The gathering got so large, we needed to break that conversation into two tables. Immediately, we saw there was an opportunity to explore how the Space Coast could develop its renewable energy assets. Within the space of a couple of hours, we were able to identify a Big Easy opportunity and define a project to move toward it. Out of that early work a new cluster of clean energy companies has formed on the Space Coast.

In making these large-scale transformations, we have learned that it does not take a large army of people to start. Our best case for illustrating that point comes with the launch of the Charleston Digital Corridor. We mentioned Charleston when we introduced the brief history of Strategic Doing. Here's more of the backstory about how the Digital Corridor came to be. Ed found his way to Charleston when the Charleston Chamber of Commerce engaged him to develop a strategic action plan for the Chamber. During one of his early trips, Ernest Andrade, a city employee contacted Ed and asked for help. Ernest had an idea, but he was unsure of how to go about implementing it. He thought Charleston could become a dynamic hub for high-growth digital businesses. In 2001, the idea seemed a bit far-fetched. Charleston had no major research university, usually an anchor for such an ambitious idea.

During their first meeting, Ed asked Ernest about his assets. He did not have much: he had the enthusiastic support of the mayor (but no new budget), and he had his logo. That was it. He made clear that he did not have money to pay for a consultant. Ed and Ernest agreed to design and launch a strategy using a monthly breakfast meeting as a 30/30. Through these meetings, Ed taught Ernest how to think about building a cluster as a portfolio of collaborative initiatives: developing talent; building supports for entrepreneurs; developing quality, connected places to make Charleston "sticky" for start-ups; and creating new narratives about the future of Charleston as a digital hub for high growth companies. Ed suggested a starting point, a Big Easy: create a monthly forum to model the behavior of collaboration that could power the Corridor forward. Ernest launched Fridays at the Corridor in 2001, and this regular meetup continues today as a central watering hole for Charleston's entrepreneurs. Today, the Charleston Digital Corridor is an internationally known ecosystem of high growth companies.

FINAL THOUGHTS

We want to finish back where we started: with the ideas in the Strategic Doing credo:

- We believe we have a responsibility to build a prosperous, sustainable future for ourselves and future generations.
- No individual, organization or place can build that future alone.
- Open, honest, focused, and caring collaboration among diverse participants is the path to accomplishing clear, valuable, shared outcomes.
- We believe in doing, not just talking – and in behavior in alignment with our beliefs.

The need for a new approach to the complex challenges in our world has never been greater. We face tremendous challenges in so many areas of our common life that describing them would fill another book and then some.

But what we also know, from our work in countless communities (only a few of which we've been able to tell you about in this book), is that while our political structures may seem permanently paralyzed, there are people in *every* community ready to roll up their sleeves, join arms with their co-workers and neighbors and get to work. They're waiting only for new ideas about how to have conversations that will lead to real change. We believe the skills in this book *are* those new ideas, and we've written it because, as the credo says, we believe in doing, not just talking. We hope you will join us in this adventure.

LEARN MORE

W e hope that your appetite has been whetted to learn more about what we view as an endlessly fascinating topic: how it is that people can most effectively work with one another to bring about change – be that in companies, organizations, communities, or regions. This final section provides some guidance on where you might head next.

Our own website, strategicdoing.net, contains a wealth of information on Strategic Doing as well as "field reports" from places in which Strategic Doing is being used. You can also find the upcoming dates for trainings to delve deeper into the skills and their application; we hold sessions across North America and as we write, we are making headway into Europe.

We've also set up a page for readers of this book at www.strategicdoing.net/skills4agile. There you'll find additional information on using the skills of agile leadership; you can also easily send us comments or questions from that page.

The following resources are arranged by chapter, including the source information for research findings or other information that we directly reference, as well as more general items that you may find helpful in exploring the topics in the chapter.

INTRODUCTION

To learn more about the history of Flint and its challenges, see:

Canapari, Z., & Cooper, D. (2018): *Flint town*. Netflix.
Highsmith, A. R. (2015). *Demolition means progress: Flint, Michigan, and the fate of the American metropolis*. University of Chicago Press.

Misjak, L. (2010). Haunted by homicides: Flint reaches 34 slayings in seven months, on pace to hit 1986 record of 61. *Flint Journal* (August 1), 2010. http://www.mlive.com/news/flint/index.ssf/2010/08/haunted_by_homicides_flint_rea.html (accessed October 19, 2018).

Crime statistics for American cities or nationally can be found on the Federal Bureau of Investigations' "Uniform Crime Reporting" portion of the agency's website: ucr.fbi.gov.

CHAPTER 1: YOU ARE HERE

Explore "satisficing" in these articles:

Simon, H. A. (1979). Rational decision making in business organizations. *American Economic Review*, 69(4), 493–513.
Simon, H. A. (1972). Theories of bounded rationality. *Decision and Organization*, 1(1), 161–176.

"Muddling through" comes from political scientist Charles Lindblom, who wrote a paper in 1959 suggesting it as the way most public policy decisions are made:

Lindblom, C. (1959). The Science of "Muddling Through." *Public Administration Review*, 19(2), 79–88. doi:10.2307/973677

Statistics on the sobering challenges to our communities and world: gun and opioid deaths, population growth, food production, and energy demands, are taken from these sources:

Alexandratos, N., & Bruinsma, J. (2012). *World agriculture towards 2030/2050: The 2012 revision* (Vol. 12, No. 3). FAO, Rome: ESA working paper.
Sieminski, A. (2014). International energy outlook. *Energy Information Administration (EIA)*, 18.
UN DES. (2017). *World population prospects: The 2075 revision: Key findings and advance tables*. United Nations.

Here are three books that explain the idea of the complex system and its role in our world:

Holland, J. H. (2014). *Complexity: A very short introduction.* Oxford University Press.
Mitchell, M. (2009). *Complexity: A guided tour.* Oxford University Press.
Waldrop, M. M. (1993). *Complexity: The emerging science at the edge of order and chaos.* Simon & Schuster.

The idea of "wicked problems" is increasingly important and discussed for the first time here:

Rittel, H. W., & Webber, M. M. (1973). Dilemmas in a general theory of planning. *Policy Sciences, 4*(2), 155–169.

Peter Drucker tells the story of the rise of management consultants in this book:

Drucker, Peter. (1974). *Management: Tasks, responsibilities, practices.* Harper & Row.

To better understand the nature and dangers of hierarchies and hierarchical thinking:

Tett, G. (2015). *The silo effect: The peril of expertise and the promise of breaking down barriers.* Simon & Schuster.

Read about the "Golden Age of Hollywood" in this dispatch from Los Angeles just as the system was beginning to change:

Hodgins, Eric. (1957). "Amid ruins of an empire a new Hollywood arises." *Life* (June 10, 1957), 146.

Our information on *The Hobbit* came from these sources:

Bulbeck, P. (2014). "'Hobbit' trilogy reportedly cost $745 million to make." *Hollywood Reporter* (October 21).
The Hobbit: An unexpected journey. (2012). The Internet Movie Database. https://www.imdb.com/title/tt0903624/ (accessed October 19, 2018).

The movie studio organization chart originally came to our attention thanks to Derek Dahlsad of the Info Mercantile, and Twentieth Century Fox has licensed its use here.

The iPod network graphic is shared courtesy of its creator, Valdis Krebs.

There has been a great deal written about social networks; there will probably be several more we could suggest by the time this book is published. Here are two we recommend:

Cross, R., Parker, A., Christensen, C. M., Anthony, S. D., & Roth, E. A. (2004). *The hidden power of social networks*. Harvard Business Press.

Cross, R. L., & Thomas, R. J. (2008). *Driving results through social networks: How top organizations leverage networks for performance and growth* (Vol. 265). Wiley.

If you're interested in how strategic planning came to be a tool of choice:

Hunter, P. (2016). *The seven inconvenient truths of business strategy*. Routledge.

Here's an explanation of why the S-Curve is critical to managing innovation:

Nunes, P., & Breene, T. (2011). *Jumping the S-curve: How to beat the growth cycle, get on top, and stay there*. Harvard Business Press. (Note: The Accenture Institute for High Performance has published a summary here: https://www.accenture.com/_acnmedia/Accenture/Conversion-Assets/DotCom/Documents/Global/PDF/Dualpub_23/Accenture-Jumping-S-Curve-POV.pdf (accessed October 19, 2018).

In both this book and in our trainings, we often lament that the word "collaboration" is surely in the "Top 10" for overuse. Nevertheless, here are several good treatments of the topic:

Chrislip, D. D., & Larson, C. E. (1994). *Collaborative leadership: How citizens and civic leaders can make a difference* (Vol. 24). Jossey-Bass.

Hansen, M. (2009). *Collaboration: How leaders avoid the traps, build common ground, and reap big results*. Harvard Business Press.

Huxham, C. (Ed.). (1996). *Creating collaborative advantage*. Sage.

You can learn about the origins of the Linux project in a video they created for the 20-year anniversary:

The Linux Foundation (2011). *The story of Linux*. https://youtu.be/ 5ocq6_3-nEw (accessed October 19, 2018).

There are, of course, many books written on the behind-the-scenes maneuvering that resulted in the US Constitution. We can recommend these:

Berkin, C. (2003). *A brilliant solution: Inventing the American Constitution*. Houghton Mifflin Harcourt.

Webb, D. A. (2012). The original meaning of civility: Democratic deliberation at the Philadelphia constitutional convention. *South Carolina Law Review, 64*, 183.

This concise description of why simple rules are so critical is a touchstone of our work:

Eisenhardt, K. M., & Sull, D. N. (2001). Strategy as simple rules. *Harvard Business Review, 79*(1), 106–119.

CHAPTER 2: SKILL 1

Amy Edmondson's work on "psychological safety" is the bedrock of this skill:

Edmondson, A. (1999). Psychological safety and learning behavior in work teams. *Administrative Science Quarterly, 44*(2), 350–383.

Read more about the idea of deep conversations here:

Mehl, M. R., Vazire, S., Holleran, S. E., & Clark, C. S. (2010). Eavesdropping on happiness: Well-being is related to having less small talk and more substantive conversations. *Psychological Science, 21*(4), 539–541.

"Equity of voice" is also a cornerstone of this skill; many of us know the principle from our own experience, but there is research behind the idea:

Keil, J., Stober, R., Quinty, E., Molloy, B., & Hooker, N. (2015). *Identifying and analyzing actions of effective group work.* Paper presented at Physics Education Research Conference 2015, College Park, MD (July 29, 2015).

The "teddy bear principle" seems almost too fantastical to be true, but for more, see:

Gino, F., & Desai, S. D. (2012). Memory lane and morality: How childhood memories promote prosocial behavior. *Journal of Personality and Social Psychology, 102*(4), 743.

Our references to optimal group size draw from these sources:

Blenko, M. W., Mankins, M. C., & Rogers, P. (2010). *Decide & deliver: 5 steps to breakthrough performance in your organization.* Harvard Business Press.
de Rond, M. (2012). Why less is more in teams. *Harvard Business Review,* 224.
Gallagher, S. M., & Leddy, C. (2017). Why most teams fail and how yours can succeed. *Influence Success.* http://www.influencesuccess.com/wp-content/uploads/2018/04/Why-Most-Teams-Fail-How-Yours-Can-Succeed.pdf (accessed October 19, 2018).
Ingham, A. G., Levinger, G., Graves, J., & Peckham, V. (1974). The Ringelmann effect: Studies of group size and group performance. *Journal of Experimental Social Psychology, 10*(4), 371–384.
Menon, T., & Williams Phillips, K. (2008). Getting even vs. being the odd one out: Conflict and cohesion in even and odd sized groups. *Organizational Science, 22*(3).

If you'd like to explore why "rapid toggling" (or multitasking) is so destructive to effectiveness, see:

Mark, G., Gudith, D., & Klocke, U. (2008, April). The cost of interrupted work: More speed and stress. In *Proceedings of the*

SIGCHI conference on Human Factors in Computing Systems
(pp. 107–110). Association for Computing Machinery.
Sullivan, B., & Thompson, H. (2013). Brain, interrupted. *New York
Times* (May 5, 2013).

Google is only one organization to put a great deal of effort into
trying to build effective teams, but we have the benefit of learning from
their experience here:

Duhigg, C. (2016). What Google learned from its quest to build the
perfect team. *New York Times Magazine*, 26, 2016.

The paradox of American democracy as a yet-to-be completely fulfilled promise is explored in these two books:

Dahl, R. A. (2003). *How democratic is the American constitution?* Yale
University Press.
Wallis, Jim (2016). *America's original sin*: Racism, White privilege, and
the bridge to a new America. Brazos Press.

CHAPTER 3: SKILL 2

The creation story of Polaroid is told in these accounts:

American Chemical Society (2015). *Edwin Land* and Polaroid photography. https://www.acs.org/content/acs/en/education/whatischem
istry/landmarks/land-instant-photography.html (accessed October
19, 2018).
McCann, M. (2012). Polaroid's instant karma. *New York Times*
(December 10, 2012).
Berger, W. (2014). *A more beautiful question: The power of inquiry to
spark breakthrough ideas*. Bloomsbury Publishing USA.

The work of Ronald Heifetz is critical to understanding the dimensions of the challenges you may be facing. Here is his seminal work on
leadership, along with a workbook to assist you in applying its lessons:

Heifetz, R. A., & Heifetz, R. (1994). *Leadership without easy answers*
(Vol. 465). Harvard University Press.

Heifetz, R. A., Grashow, A., & Linsky, M. (2009). *The practice of adaptive leadership: Tools and tactics for changing your organization and the world*. Harvard Business Press.

Rather than refer you to only one source on Appreciative Inquiry, David Cooperrider's website is full of helpful information:

www.davidcooperrider.com

Tina Seelig's elegant explanation of the essence of a powerful question is from her book:

Seelig, T. (2012). *inGenius: A crash course on creativity*. Hay House.

The idea of a "mental model" comes from the work of (among others) Philip Johnson-Laird:

Johnson-Laird, P. N. (1980). Mental models in cognitive science. *Cognitive Science*, 4(1), 71–115.

For the backstory on how Steve Jobs posed the right question to (arguably) launch our digital age, see:

Palus, C. J., & Horth, D. M. (2002). *The leader's edge: Six creative competencies for navigating complex challenges*. Jossey-Bass.

Gervase R. Bushe has graciously given us permission to use his checklist for good questions, found here:

Bushe, G. (2007). Appreciative inquiry is not (just) about the positive. *OD Practitioner*, 39(4), 33–38.

CHAPTER 4: SKILL 3

The idea of basing strategy on assets got its start in community development; for more, see:

Nurture Development. http://www.nurturedevelopment.org/asset-based-community-development/ (accessed October 19, 2018).

We're not the first to draw business lessons from the art of improvisation, as you'll read here:

Barrett, F. (2012). *Yes to the mess: Surprising leadership lessons from jazz*. Harvard Business Press.

CHAPTER 5: SKILL 4

The Caesar salad is iconic in part because of its fascinating origin story:

Henderson, P. (2014). Caesar salad turns 90? *San Diego Reader* (July 4, 2014).

Recombinant innovation in the food world is explored in this article from a journal having nothing to do with cuisine:

Messeni Petruzzelli, A., & Savino, T. (2015). Reinterpreting tradition to innovate: The case of Italian haute cuisine. *Industry and Innovation*, 22(8), 677–702.

Explore the idea of horizontal thinking here:

Burke, J. (1995). *Connections: From Ptolemy's astrolabe to the discovery of electricity, how inventions are linked and how they cause change throughout history*. Little, Brown and Company (revised, 1995).

Johansson, F., (2006). *The Medici effect: What elephants and epidemics can teach us about innovation*. Harvard Business School Press

Johnson, S. (2011). *Where good ideas come from: The seven patterns of innovation*. Penguin UK.

Learn more about the infusion pump innovation here:

Fiorini, P. (2012). Regenstrief launches hospital research community to improve infusion pump drug-delivery system. *Purdue News Service* (July 16, 2012).

The idea that groups using horizontal thinking create an "extended mind" comes from these sources:

Clark, A., & Chalmers, D. (1998). The extended mind. *Analysis*, 58(1), 7–19.
Sloman, S., & Fernbach, P. (2018). *The knowledge illusion: Why we never think alone*. Penguin.

The story of how bears and honey helped an engineer on a thought walk solve a technical problem is described on Michael Michalko's fascinating website:

creativethinking.net

For more on our brains and creativity, see:

Mednick, S. (1962). The associative basis of the creative process. *Psychological Review*, 69(3), 220.

CHAPTER 6: SKILL 5

The role trust plays in a how a decision process is perceived is explored in these sources:

Daellenbach, U. S., & Davenport, S. J. (2004). Establishing trust during the formation of technology alliances. *Journal of Technology Transfer*, 29(2), 187–202.
Korsgaard, M. A., Schweiger, D. M., & Sapienza, H. J. (1995). Building commitment, attachment, and trust in strategic decision-making teams: The role of procedural justice. *Academy of Management Journal*, 38(1), 60–84.
Tackx, K., Van der Heyden, L., & Verdin, P. (2016). *Fairness in strategy: A fair process evaluation of strategy schools* (working paper). Université Libre de Bruxelles—Solvay Brussels School of Economics and Management.

The 2x2 matrix is a powerful tool, as these authors make clear:

Lowy, A., & Hood, P. (2011). *The power of the 2×2 matrix: Using 2×2 thinking to solve business problems and make better decisions.* Wiley.

Stanford's Katherine Eisenhart explains the concept of group intuition here:

Eisenhardt, K. M. (1999). Strategy as strategic decision making. *Sloan Management Review, 40*(3), 65–72.

CHAPTER 7: SKILL 6

The idea of prospection ("reminiscing forward") is a fascinating one; for more, see:

Gilbert, D. T., & Wilson, T. D. (2007). Prospection: Experiencing the future. *Science, 317*(5843), 1351–1354.

In writing the book, members of our team expressed skepticism about being able to "see" dopamine activity; if you are doubtful as well, read more here:

Lee, T., Cai, L. X., Lelyveld, V. S., Hai, A., & Jasanoff, A. (2014). Molecular-level functional magnetic resonance imaging of dopaminergic signaling. *Science, 344*(6183), 533–535.

CHAPTER 8: SKILL 7

Our understanding of the idea of small successes draws from these sources:

Amabile, T. M., & Kramer, S. J. (2011). The power of small wins. *Harvard Business Review, 89*(5), 70–80.

Diaz, P. P. (2012). The progress principle: Using small wins to ignite joy, engagement, and creativity at work. *Research Technology Management, 55*(6), 68.

Schlesinger, L., & Kiefer, C. (2012). *Just start: Take action, embrace uncertainty, create the future.* Harvard Business Review Press.

Weick, K. E. (1984). Small wins: Redefining the scale of social problems. *American Psychologist, 39*(1), 40.

We've used several terms to describe your team's initial work or starting project, based on these researchers' work:

Gerber, E., & Carroll, M. (2012). The psychological experience of prototyping. *Design Studies, 33*(1), 64–84

Harford, T. (2011). *Adapt: Why success always starts with failure.* Farrar, Straus and Giroux.

Liedtka, J. (2009). *Designing learning launches.* Darden Business Publishing, University of Virginia.

CHAPTER 9: SKILL 8

Read more about Amy Edmondson's work on "teaming" in this book:

Edmondson, A. C. (2012). *Teaming: How organizations learn, innovate, and compete in the knowledge economy.* Wiley.

Explore the dimensions of shared leadership in these resources:

Goldsmith, M. (2010, May 26). Shared leadership to maximize talent. *Harvard Business Review.*

The concept of "promise-based management" as a prerequisite for shared leadership comes from this article:

D'Innocenzo, L., Mathieu, J. E., & Kukenberger, M. R. (2016). A meta-analysis of different forms of shared leadership–team performance relations. *Journal of Management, 42*(7), 1964–1991.

Sull, D. N., & Spinosa, C. (2007). Promise-based management. *Harvard Business Review, 85*(4), 79–86.

Wang, D., Waldman, D. A., & Zhang, Z. (2013). A meta-analysis of shared leadership and team effectiveness. *Journal of Applied Psychology*, 99(2): 181–198.

"Micro-commitments" form the basis of this skill; these resources explore the idea, although without using the term:

Brinkmann, K. (2017). How to raise teachers' motivation through "nudges" and attribution theory. *Open Journal of Social Sciences*, 5, 11–20.

Cheng, J., Kulkarni, C., & Klemmer, S. (2013). Tools for predicting drop-off in large online classes. *Proceedings of the 2013 Conference on Computer Supported Cooperative Work Companion — CSCW '13*, 121–124.

Jamison, J., & Wegener, J. (2010). Multiple selves in intertemporal choice. *Journal of Economic Psychology*, 832–839.

If you, too, have a dissertation that needs to be finished up, we're happy to share this useful volume:

Bolker, J. (1998). *Writing your dissertation in fifteen minutes a day: A guide to starting, revising, and finishing your doctoral thesis*. Holt Paperbacks.

If you'd like to read more about the Epicenter project with 50 universities, here are the relevant articles:

Nilsen, E., & Morrison, E. F., & Asencio, R., & Hutcheson, S. (2017, June). *Getting "There": Understanding how innovation and entrepreneurship become part of engineering education*. Paper presented at 2017 ASEE Annual Conference & Exposition, Columbus, Ohio. https://peer.asee.org/28404 (accessed October 19, 2018).

Nilsen, E., & Monroe-White, T., & Morrison, E. F., & Weilerstein, P. (2016, June). *Going beyond "What Should We Do?": An approach to implementation of innovation and entrepreneurship in the curriculum*. Paper presented at 2016 ASEE Annual Conference & Exposition, New Orleans, Louisiana. https://peer.asee.org/25405 (accessed October 19, 2018).

Finally, while not referenced directly in the book, we've found several other works helpful in exploring this skill:

Collins, J. (2007). Level 5 leadership. *The Jossey-Bass reader on educational leadership* (2nd ed.), pp. 27–50. Jossey Bass.

Greenleaf, R. K. (2002). *Servant leadership: A journey into the nature of legitimate power and greatness.* Paulist Press.

Haiman. F. S. (1951). *Group leadership and democratic action.* Houghton-Mifflin.

Hersey, P., Blanchard, K. H., & Johnson, D. E. (2007). *Management of organizational behavior* (Vol. 9). Prentice Hall.

CHAPTER 10: SKILL 9

Chris Argyris is the premier thinker about organizational learning; here are a few of his resources:

Argyris, C. (2000). Teaching smart people how to learn. In R. Cross, Jr. & S. Israelit (Eds.), *Strategic learning in a knowledge economy* (pp. 279–296). Elsevier.

Argyris, C. (2002). Double-loop learning, teaching, and research. *Academy of Management Learning & Education, 1*(2), 206–218.

Argyris is not the only person who's explored this theme, however; here is another source we've found useful;

Richardson, J. (2014). Double loop learning: A powerful force for organizational excellence. In *Proceedings of the Pacific Northwest Software Quality Conference.*

While it covers history before the Shoals Shift Project, we can't pass up the opportunity to recommend this documentary about the music industry around Muscle Shoals, Alabama:

Camalier, G., & Badger, S. (2013). *Muscle Shoals.* Magnolia Pictures.

CHAPTER 11: SKILL 10

There is an entire book about the idea of "nudging":

Thaler, R. H., & Sunstein, C. R. (2008). *Nudge: Improving decisions about health, wealth, and happiness.* Yale University Press.

The example of nudging to influence retirement savings is told here:

Ben-Artzi, S., & Thaler, R. H. (2013). Behavioral economics and the retirement savings crisis. *Science, 339*(6124), 1152–1153.

Utkus, S. (2002). A recent successful test of the SMarT program. *Vanguard Center for Retirement Research*. September 2002. Available at https://institutional.vanguard.com/pdf/SMarT_112002.pdf

There are also these more granular pieces of advice about how to effectively nudge in the digital age:

Halpern, D. (2016). *Inside the nudge unit: How small changes can make a big difference*. Random House.

Shamah, D. (2015). The fine art and gentle science of digital nudging *The Times of Israel*, December 22, 2015.

We often refer to nudging as the primary tool to "build trust at scale." Here are three of the most illuminating resources we've found on trust:

Blacksher, E., Nelson, C., Van Dyke, E., Echo-Hawk, A., Bassett, D., & Buchwald, D. (2016). Conversations about community-based participatory research and trust: "We Are Explorers Together." *Progress in Community Health Partnerships: Research, Education, and Action*.

Christopher, S., Watts, V., McCormick, A.K.H. G., & Young, S. (2008). Building and maintaining trust in a community-based participatory research partnership. *American Journal of Public Health*.

Fukuyama, F. (1995). *Trust: The social virtues and the creation of prosperity* (No. D10 301 c. 1/c. 2). Free Press Paperbacks.

CHAPTER 12: TEN SKILLS. GOT IT. NOW WHAT?

The detailed explanation of how Benjamin Franklin made decisions is described here:

From Benjamin Franklin to Joseph Priestly, 19 September 1772. *Founders Online*, https://founders.archives.gov/?q=Franklin%20Priestly&s=1111311111&sa=&r=24&sr= (accessed October 19, 2018).

If you'd like to read more about "requisite variety," see this article:

Ashby, W. R., & Goldstein, J. (2011). Variety, constraint, and the law of requisite variety. *Emergence: Complexity and Organization, 13*(1/2), 190.

We believe the idea of "cognitive diversity" will take on increasing importance in the coming years; here's one source to learn more:

Page, S. (2007). *The difference: How the power of diversity creates better groups, firms, schools, and societies.* Princeton University Press.

We have found the AEM-Cube® to be a remarkable tool for helping teams explore their cognitive and strategic diversity, understand their strengths and build for growth. You can learn more about the tool here:

agilestrategylab.org (in North America)
human-insight.com (elsewhere)

These articles also provide helpful background on the tool:

Robertson, P. P. (2005). *Always change a winning team.* Marshall Cavendish Business.
Reynolds, A., & Lewis, D. (2017, March 30). Teams solve problems faster when they're more cognitively diverse. *Harvard Business Review.*

If you've ever wondered how it is that, for example, birds know how to fly together in tight formation, you'll enjoy this explanation of how simple rules make such complex collaborations possible:

Johnson, S. (2002). *Emergence: The connected lives of ants, brains, cities, and software.* Simon & Schuster.

The Drucker quote on finding the right question can be found here:

Drucker, P. F. (1954). *The practice of management: A study of the most important function in America society.* Harper & Brothers.

BIBLIOGRAPHY

Alexandratos, N., & Bruinsma, J. (2012). *World agriculture towards 2030/2050: The 2012 revision* (Vol. 12, No. 3). FAO, Rome: ESA working paper.

Amabile, T. M., & Kramer, S. J. (2011). The power of small wins. *Harvard Business Review*, 89(5), 70–80.

American Chemical Society (2015). *Edwin Land and Polaroid photography*. https://www.acs.org/content/acs/en/education/whatischemistry/landmarks/land-instant-photography.html (accessed October 19, 2018).

Argyris, C. (2002). Double-loop learning, teaching, and research. *Academy of Management Learning & Education*, 1(2), 206–218.

Ashby, W. R., & Goldstein, J. (2011). Variety, constraint, and the law of requisite variety. *Emergence: Complexity and Organization*, 13(1/2), 190.

Ben-Artzi, S., & Thaler, R. H. (2013). Behavioral economics and the retirement savings crisis. *Science*, 339(6124), 1152–1153.

Berkin, C. (2003). *A brilliant solution: Inventing the American Constitution*. Houghton Mifflin Harcourt.

Blenko, M. W., Mankins, M. C., & Rogers, P. (2010). *Decide & deliver: 5 steps to breakthrough performance in your organization*. Harvard Business Press.

Bolker, J. (1998). *Writing your dissertation in fifteen minutes a day: A guide to starting, revising, and finishing your doctoral thesis*. Holt Paperbacks.

Bulbeck, P. (2014). "Hobbit" trilogy reportedly cost $745 million to make. *Hollywood Reporter* (October 21).

Burke, J. (1995). *Connections: From Ptolemy's astrolabe to the discovery of electricity, how inventions are linked and how they cause change throughout history*. Little, Brown and Company (revised, 1995).

Bushe, G. Appreciative inquiry is not (just) about the positive (2007). *OD Practitioner, 39*(4), 33–38.

Clark, A., & Chalmers, D. (1998). The extended mind. *Analysis, 58*(1), 7–19.

Dahl, R. A. (2003). *How democratic is the American constitution?* Yale University Press.

de Rond, M. (2012). Why less is more in teams. *Harvard Business Review, 224.*

D'Innocenzo, L., Mathieu, J. E., & Kukenberger, M. R. (2016). A meta-analysis of different forms of shared leadership–team performance relations. *Journal of Management, 42*(7), 1964–1991.

Diaz, P. P. (2012). The progress principle: Using small wins to ignite joy, engagement, and creativity at work. *Research Technology Management, 55*(6), 68.

Drucker, P. F. (1954). *The practice of management: A study of the most important function in America society.* Harper & Brothers.

Duhigg, C. (2016). What Google learned from its quest to build the perfect team. *New York Times Magazine, 26,* 2016.

Edmondson, A. (1999). Psychological safety and learning behavior in work teams. *Administrative Science Quarterly, 44*(2), 350–383.

Edmondson, A. C. (2012). *Teaming: How organizations learn, innovate, and compete in the knowledge economy.* Wiley.

Eisenhardt, K. M. (1999). Strategy as strategic decision making. *Sloan Management Review, 40*(3), 65–72.

Eisenhardt, K. M., & Sull, D. N. (2001). Strategy as simple rules. *Harvard Business Review, 79*(1), 106–119.

Fiorini, P. (2012). "Regenstrief launches hospital research community to improve infusion pump drug-delivery system." *Purdue News Service* (July 16, 2012).

Franklin, B. (1772). From Benjamin Franklin to Joseph Priestly, 19 September 1772, *Founders Online,* https://founders.archives .gov/?q=Franklin%20Priestly&s=1111311111&sa=&r=24&sr= (accessed October 19, 2018).

Henderson, P. (2014). Caesar salad turns 90? *San Diego Reader* (July 4, 2014).

Gallagher, S. M., & Leddy, C. (2017). Why most teams fail and how yours can succeed. *Influence Success*. http://www.influencesuccess .com/wp-content/uploads/2018/04/Why-Most-Teams-Fail-How-Yours-Can-Succeed.pdf (accessed October 19, 2018).

Gerber, E., & Carroll, M. (2012). The psychological experience of prototyping. *Design Studies, 33*(1), 64–84

Gilbert, D. T., & Wilson, T. D. (2007). Prospection: Experiencing the future. *Science, 317*(5843), 1351–1354.

Gino, F., & Desai, S. D. (2012). Memory lane and morality: How childhood memories promote prosocial behavior. *Journal of Personality and Social Psychology, 102*(4), 743.

Goldsmith, M. (2010). *Shared leadership to maximize talent*. Harvard Business Review.

Halpern, D. (2016). *Inside the nudge unit: How small changes can make a big difference*. Random House.

Harford, T. (2011). *Adapt: Why success always starts with failure*. Farrar, Straus and Giroux.

Heifetz, R. A., & Heifetz, R. (1994). *Leadership without easy answers* (Vol. 465). Harvard University Press.

Highsmith, A. R. (2015). *Demolition means progress: Flint, Michigan, and the fate of the American metropolis*. University of Chicago Press.

The Hobbit: An unexpected journey. (2012). Retrieved from The Internet Movie Database. https://www.imdb.com/title/tt0903624/ (accessed October 19, 2018).

Ingham, A. G., Levinger, G., Graves, J., & Peckham, V. (1974). The Ringelmann effect: Studies of group size and group performance. *Journal of Experimental Social Psychology, 10*(4), 371–384.

Johansson, F, (2006). *The Medici effect: What elephants and epidemics can teach us about innovation*. Harvard Business School Press.

Johnson, S. (2011). *Where good ideas come from: the seven patterns of innovation*. Penguin UK.

Johnson-Laird, P. N. (1980). Mental models in cognitive science. *Cognitive Science, 4*(1), 71–115.

Keil, J., Stober, R., Quinty, E., Molloy, B., & Hooker, N. (2015). *Identifying and analyzing actions of effective group work.* Paper presented at Physics Education Research Conference 2015, College Park, MD (July 29, 2015).

Krebs, Valdis (n.d.). *iPhone development network.* Provided by creator.

Lee, T., Cai, L. X., Lelyveld, V. S., Hai, A., & Jasanoff, A. (2014). Molecular-level functional magnetic resonance imaging of dopaminergic signaling. *Science, 344*(6183), 533–535.

Liedtka, J. (2009). *Designing learning launches.* Darden Business Publishing, University of Virginia.

Lindblom, C. (1959). The science of "Muddling Through." *Public Administration Review, 19*(2), 79–88. doi:10.2307/973677

Lowy, A., & Hood, P. (2011). *The power of the 2×2 matrix: Using 2×2 thinking to solve business problems and make better decisions.* Wiley.

Mark, G., Gudith, D., & Klocke, U. (2008, April). The cost of interrupted work: More speed and stress. In *Proceedings of the SIGCHI conference on Human Factors in Computing Systems* (pp. 107–110). Association for Computing Machinery.

McCann, M. (2012). Polaroid's instant karma. *New York Times* (December 10, 2012).

Mednick, S. (1962). The associative basis of the creative process. *Psychological Review, 69*(3), 220.

Mehl, M. R., Vazire, S., Holleran, S. E., & Clark, C. S. (2010). Eavesdropping on happiness: Well-being is related to having less small talk and more substantive conversations. *Psychological Science, 21*(4), 539–541.

Menon, T., & Williams Phillips, K. (2008). Getting even vs. being the odd one out: Conflict and cohesion in even and odd sized groups. *Organizational Science, 22*(3).

Messeni Petruzzelli, A., & Savino, T. (2015). Reinterpreting tradition to innovate: The case of Italian haute cuisine. *Industry and Innovation, 22*(8), 677–702.

Michalko, Michael. (n.d.). *The story of the thought walk.* creativethinking.net (accessed October 29, 2018).

Misjak, L. (2010). Haunted by homicides: Flint reaches 34 slayings in seven months, on pace to hit 1986 record of 61. *Flint Journal* (August 1) 2010. http://www.mlive.com/news/flint/index.ssf/2010/08/haunted_by_homicides_flint_rea.html (accessed October 19, 2018).

Nilsen, E., & Morrison, E. F., & Asencio, R., & Hutcheson, S. (2017, June), *Getting "There": Understanding how innovation and entrepreneurship become part of engineering education*. Paper presented at 2017 ASEE Annual Conference & Exposition, Columbus, Ohio. https://peer.asee.org/28404 (accessed October 19, 2018).

Palus, C. J., & Horth, D. M. (2002). *The leader's edge: Six creative competencies for navigating complex challenges*. Jossey-Bass.

Rittel, H. W., & Webber, M. M. (1973). Dilemmas in a general theory of planning. *Policy Sciences*, 4(2), 155–169.

Schlesinger, L., & Kiefer, C. (2012). *Just start: Take action, embrace uncertainty, create the future*. Harvard Business Review Press.

Seelig, T. (2012). *inGenius: A crash course on creativity*. Hay House.

Shamah, D. (2015, December 22). The fine art and gentle science of digital nudging. *Times of Israel*.

Simon, H. A. (1979). Rational decision making in business organizations. *American Economic Review*, 69(4), 493–513.

Sloman, S., & Fernbach, P. (2018). *The knowledge illusion: Why we never think alone*. Penguin.

Sieminski, A. (2014). International energy outlook. *Energy Information Administration (EIA)*, 18.

Sull, D. N., & Spinosa, C. (2007). Promise-based management. *Harvard Business Review*, 85(4), 79–86.

Sullivan, B., & Thompson, H. (2013) Brain, interrupted. *New York Times* (May 5, 2013).

Tackx, K., Van der Heyden, L., & Verdin, P. (2016). *Fairness in strategy: A fair process evaluation of strategy schools* (working paper). Université Libre de Bruxelles—Solvay Brussels School of Economics and Management.

Thaler, R. H., Sunstein, C. R. (2008). *Nudge: Improving decisions about health, wealth, and happiness*. Yale University Press.

Twentieth Century Fox (n.d.). *Studio organization chart*. Provided by studio.

UN DES. (2017). *World population prospects: The 2075 revision: Key findings and advance tables*. United Nations.

Utkus, S. (2002). A recent successful test of the SMarT program. *Vanguard Center for Retirement Research*. September 2002. Available at https://institutional.vanguard.com/pdf/SMarT_112002.pdf (accessed October 29, 2018).

Wallis, Jim (2016). *America's original sin: Racism, white privilege, and the bridge to a new America*. Brazos Press.

Wang, D., Waldman, D. A., & Zhang, Z. (2013). A meta-analysis of shared leadership and team effectiveness. *Journal of Applied Psychology*, 99(2): 181–198.

Webb, D. A. (2012). The original meaning of civility: Democratic deliberation at the Philadelphia constitutional convention. *South Carolina Law Review*, 64, 183.

Weick, K. E. (1984). Small wins: Redefining the scale of social problems. *American Psychologist*, 39(1), 40.

ACKNOWLEDGMENTS

O ne of the core messages of this book is that transformations are possible only through collaboration. That principle is no less true of Strategic Doing itself – it has been continuously refined by the people who have used it, from the kernel of an idea more than two decades ago to a discipline that is taught throughout the United States and Canada (and is beginning to make its impact felt elsewhere as well). Our first thanks go to this growing "community of practice." While these additional acknowledgments are certainly not all-inclusive, we want to especially express our gratitude to the following:

The leaders in Oklahoma City, Kentucky, and Charleston, whose communities served as the initial proving grounds for Strategic Doing: Charles Van Rysselberge, Clay Bennett, Burns Hargis, J. R. Wilhite, and Ernest Andrade.

The core team in Flint, which has taught us that Strategic Doing can make a difference in confronting truly life-and-death issues: Bob Brown, Kenyetta Dotson, Alexis Murphy Morris, Hubert Roberts, Artina Sadler, Donna Ulrich, and the much-missed Tendaji Ganges.

Peggy Hosea, who worked with the Purdue team for more than a decade and created the systems that ensured our work led to success, while laying the groundwork to build out a global network of practitioners and partner institutions.

Nina Wojtalewicz, who's kept the plates spinning at the Agile Strategy Lab so that Ed, Scott, and Liz could find the time to write.

The team at Wiley, for their guidance to our team of novices; we are grateful to Jeanenne Ray, Vicki Adang, and Beula Jaculin, as well as all those behind the scenes.

Kim Mitchell of Community Renewal International in Shreveport, Louisiana; Kim turned his tremendous visual communication skills to our work several years ago — beginning with a session in which he and Ed locked themselves in a conference room with a whiteboard and lots of markers. The graphics have been refined over the years (including a new "streamlined" look by David Allen Moss of MossMedia) but remain a vital part of our teaching.

Our fellow members on the Strategic Doing core team: Bob Brown, Rena Cotsones, Tim Franklin, Michon Hicks, and Janet Holston.

The faculty and staff at Purdue who have invited us into their work to take on audacious challenges across many disciplines. There is no way to list them all, but in particular we want to thank the leaders that have supported the growth of our work there: Ken Burbank, Sam Cordes, Duane Dunlap, Vic Lechtenberg, and former president Martin Jischke.

David Cooperrider, whose pioneering work in Appreciative Inquiry has unlocked the power of groups to create new futures for their organizations and communities, and has made all of our strategic conversations possible.

Finally, while he is no longer with us, we are grateful to David Morgenthaler, one of Ed's mentors. As Ed was working to make sense of a new approach to strategy, it was David who first suggested using S-Curves to explain the transformation. An iconic investor, David founded Morgenthaler Ventures and was a pioneer in the venture capital industry. He generously shared his time and expertise, and he spent the last years of his life "paying it forward" in so many ways.

ABOUT THE AUTHORS

Ed Morrison (JD/MBA) directs the Agile Strategy Lab at Purdue University. He pioneered the development of a new approach to strategy and complex collaboration in open, loosely connected networks. Prior to joining Purdue, he conducted strategy projects throughout the United States and China. His work won the first Arthur D. Little Award presented by the American Economic Development Council. Ed started his professional career in Washington, DC, where he served as a legislative assistant on Capitol Hill, staff attorney in the Federal Trade Commission, and staff counsel in the US Senate. He has served several terms on the board of directors of the University Economic Development Association.

Scott Hutcheson (PhD) is associate director of the Agile Strategy Lab at Purdue University and a faculty member in Purdue University's School of Engineering Technology. His focus is on agile approaches to strategy and the science of collaboration. His writing has been published in academic journals, books, newspapers, magazines, and he has also written and produced short documentaries for television. Scott has received two best-column awards from the Hoosier State Press Association, a Best Creative Nonfiction award from the Indiana State Library's Center for the Book, and his work for WFYI Public Television in Indianapolis was nominated for two Emmys.

Elizabeth Nilsen (MBA) is senior program director of the Agile Strategy Lab at Purdue University. Her background includes leadership of science, technology, engineering, and math (STEM) initiatives at local, regional, and state levels, as well as work with a number of higher education change initiatives. Her nonprofit experience includes program design and management, fundraising, operations, and executive leadership. Liz has authored a number of research articles as well as publications for organizations seeking to address issues of community vitality.

Janyce Fadden (MBA) is director of strategic engagement at the University of North Alabama, where she is the principal architect of Shoals Shift, a regional innovation initiative, which won a 2016 award from the University Economic Development Association and was a finalist for the 2018 Phi Kappa Phi Innovation Award. Janyce has an extensive private sector background, including leadership positions at Honeywell, General Signal, and Danaher Corporation, and serves on the board of directors for the Shoals Chamber of Commerce.

Nancy Franklin (EdD), principal of Franklin Solutions, collaborates with leaders of higher education, government, and business to facilitate strategic partnerships, innovation initiatives, talent development, agile planning, and program creation. Previously, she led strategic initiatives in community–university engagement and technology in teaching and learning at Virginia Tech, Penn State, and Indiana State University after an early career with IBM and ROLM. Nancy has been inducted into the Academy of Community Engagement Scholars and currently serves on the University of Pennsylvania Executive Doctorate Alumni Advisory Board.

INDEX

There are a number of terms that are used so frequently throughout the book that this index does not attempt to capture them all – only the most critical or illustrative are included in the index. Those terms include: "collaboration," "conversation," "network," "guiding," and "Strategic Doing."